Words of Advice Regarding Da'wah

from the noble Shaykh

'Abdul 'Azeez ibn 'Abdullaah ibn Baaz

Compiled by
Ziyaad ibn Muhammad as-Sa'doon

Translated by
Bint Feroz Deen & Bint 'Abd al-Ghafoor

ISBN 1 898649 28 6

British Library Cataloguing in Publication Data.

A catalogue record for this book is available from the British Library.

First Edition, 1418 AH/1998 CE

Cover design: Abu Yahya

Typeset by: Al-Hidaayah Publishing and Distribution

Printed by: Alltrade Printers, Birmingham
Tel: 0121 359 2346

Published by: Al-Hidaayah Publishing and Distribution
P.O. Box 3332
Birmingham
United Kingdom
B10 9AW

Tel: 0121 753 1889
Fax: 0121 753 2422
E-Mail: ahpd@hidaayah.demon.co.uk

Contents

Transliteration Table

Consonants

ء	'		ض	d
ب	b		ط	t
ت	t		ظ	dh
ث	th		ع	'
ج	j		غ	gh
ح	h		ف	f
خ	kh		ق	q
د	d		ك	k
ذ	dh		ل	l
ر	r		م	m
ز	z		ن	n
س	s		ه	h
ش	sh		و	w
ص	s		ي	y

Vowels

َ	a		َا	aa
ُ	u		ُو	oo
ِ	i		ِي	ee

Compiler's Forward*

All praise is for Allaah. We praise Him, we seek His aid and we ask for His forgiveness. We seek Allaah's refuge from the evils or ourselves and the evils of our actions. Whomsoever Allaah guides, there is no one to misguide him and whomsoever Allaah misguides, there is no one to guide him. I testify that none has the right to be worshipped except Allaah, alone, who has no partner and I testify that Muhammad (ﷺ) is His slave and Messenger.

To proceed.

It is well known that the call *(da'wah)* to Allaah is one of the most important matters in the religion. The one who wants to succeed in his call *(da'wah)* to Allaah must be careful to know who he takes his religion from.

The one who researches and reflects over the Islamic movements and *da'wah* organisations of the past and present times will learn that the greatest causes of their failure and deviation from the straight path in *da'wah* are:

(i) their error with regards to the source of their knowledge and guidance;

(ii) their disregard of religious knowledge; and

(iii) their distance from the advice of the scholars.

Out of desire to partake in preserving this (current) blessed awakening which we are witnessing and to firmly establish it upon the

---

* Slightly adapted.

statements of the scholars in order for it to bear fruit. I have started this series with one of these reformist scholars. He himself has practised *da'wah* for many years by teaching, giving legal rulings and giving guidance through lectures and conferences. His words are of great importance because of his abundant knowledge of the *Sharee'ah* and great experience in *da'wah*. He is none other than the honourable Shaykh 'Abdul 'Azeez Ibn 'Abdullaah Ibn Baaz, the *imaam* of the callers to Islaam in this age, may Allaah preserve him. These pieces of advice and guidance are spread throughout the book of the Shaykh, called 'A Collection of Various *Fataawa* (Legal Rulings) and Articles'. I have compiled it and classified it into subheadings in order to make it accessible to anyone who wants to read it and to turn it into a manual which will benefit the *daa'ees* and reformers.

As you know my honourable brother, gathering and classifying a piece of work is easy, and what I have done here doesn't mean that I have a lot of knowledge or that I am a person of great resolve.

I ask Allaah, the Most High, to reward the honourable Shaykh for what he has done for this *Ummah*, to bless this awakening, to unite the hearts upon good, to reward the good doers because of their good deeds, to forgive those who commit errors while they are sincere and make us happy with the victory of Islaam and the supremacy of the Muslims.

In view of the fact that the book, 'A Collection of Various *Fataawa* and Articles', has been published several times, the edition I have referred to is the second edition which was printed for The Society of Preserving the Noble Qur'aan. May the peace and blessings of Allaah be upon our Prophet (ﷺ), his family and his Companions.

Ziyaad ibn Muhammad as-Sa'doon

A Brief Biography of the Author

His Name

'Abdul Azeez Ibn 'Abdullaah Ibn 'Abdur-Rahmaan Ibn Muhammad Ibn 'Abdullaah Aal Baaz.

His Birth

He was born in the year 1330H in the city of Riyaad, Saudi Arabia. He had normal sight at the beginning of his studies and was than afflicted with an illness in 1346H which impaired his eyesight. He later became blind in 1350H when he was only 20 years old.

Seeking Knowledge

He started upon the path of knowledge at a young age and memorised the Qur'aan before puberty. The Shaykh excelled in his knowledge of the various branches of the *Sharee'ah* and the Arabic language and was then appointed as a judge. This however, did not stop him from seeking knowledge until this present day. The various offices he has held and still holds have not prevented him from teaching and engaging in research.

His Teachers

1. Shaykh Muhammad Ibn 'Abdul-Lateef Ibn 'Abdur-Rahmaan Ibn Hasan Ibn As-Shaykh Muhammad ibn 'Abdul-Wahhaab, may Allaah have mercy upon them all.

2. Shaykh Sa'd Ibn Hamad Ibn 'Ateeq (The Chief Judge of Riyaad).

3. Hamad Ibn Faaris (Vice Chancellor of the Treasury at Riyaad).

4. Shaykh Saalih Ibn 'Abdul-'Azeez Ibn 'Abdur-Rahmaan Ibn Hasan Ibn Shaykh Muhammad Ibn 'Abdul-Wahhaab (The Chief Judge of Riyaad).

5. Sa'd Waqqaas, al-Bukhaaree, one of the scholars of Makkah who he learnt the science of *tajweed* from in the year 1355H.

6. Shaykh Muhammad Ibn Ibraaheem Ibn 'Abdul-Lateef Aal Ash-Shaykh. The (former) official expounder of law in Saudi Arabia. Shaykh Ibn Baaz attended and adhered to his study circles for approximately ten years. He learnt all the branches of the *Sharee'ah* from him from the year 1347H up until 1357H whereupon his teacher then nominated him for a post in the judiciary.

His Various Posts and Positions Held

1. Judge in Al-Kharaj district for a lengthy time, spanning approximately 14 years from 1357H till 1371H.

2. Teaching post in Riyaadh at *al-Ma'had Al-'Ilmee* in 1372H then to the college of *Sharee'ah* from it's inception in 1373H. He taught the sciences of *Fiqh*, *Tawheed* and *Hadeeth*. This continued for nine years up until 1380H.

3. He was appointed as Vice-Chancellor of the Islamic University of Madeenah in the year 1381H and he remained in this post until 1390H.

4. He became Chancellor of the University in 1390H upon the death of the then Chancellor Shaykh Muhammad Ibn Ibraheem Aal As-Shaykh may Allaah have mercy upon him. He remained Chancellor until 1395H.

5. In 1413H, he was appointed as the official expounder of Law in Saudi Arabia in addition to presidency of the committee of senior

scholars and presidency of the administration for scientific research and legal rulings.

To this present time he is a member of many other Islamic Committees, such as:

1. President of the Permanent Committee for Scientific Research and Legal Rulings.

2. President and member of the Constituent Assembly of the World Muslim League.

3. President of the Higher World League Council.

4. President of the Islamic *Fiqh* Assembly based at Makkah which is a subsidiary council to the Muslim World League.

5. Member of the Higher Council of the Islamic University of Madeenah.

6. Member of the Higher Committee for Islamic *Da'wah* in Saudi Arabia.

His Influence

The Shaykh has influenced and effected many people and in many different ways. An important way was via the study circles and lectures he delivered and is still delivering up until this day. These date back from the days he used to reside in the Al-Kharaj district, then in the various educational establishments he taught in whether in Riyaad̲ or at the University or the Prophet's Mosque in Madeenah.

He still has a study circle at the mosque *Al-Jaami' Al-Kabeer* in Riyaad̲.

Chapter 1.
The Excellence of *Da'wah* and Those Who Give *Da'wah*.

Anyone who has the least amount of knowledge, knows about the excellence of *da'wah* and that it is a great matter, and that it was the mission of the Messengers, *'alayhimus-salaam.*

Allaah has raised the status of the *daa'ees* (the people calling to Islaam) and He has praised them and commended them very highly.

Allaah says in the Qur'aan,

وَمَنْ أَحْسَنُ قَوْلًا مِّمَّن دَعَآ إِلَى ٱللَّهِ وَعَمِلَ صَٰلِحًا وَقَالَ إِنَّنِى مِنَ ٱلْمُسْلِمِينَ ﴿٣٣﴾

Who is better in speech than the one who calls to Allaah, does righteous deeds and says indeed I am from the Muslims.[1]

There is no doubt that this praise serves to motivate ones determination, stirs up ones feelings, lightens the burden of *da'wah* (which one may feel) and calls one to race along in the interest of *da'wah* with all of ones strength and vitality. It has been reported by 'Abdul-Razzaaq on the authority of Ma'moor, on the authority of Hasan al-Basree, may Allaah have mercy on him, that he recited this verse,

وَمَنْ أَحْسَنُ قَوْلًا مِّمَّن دَعَآ إِلَى ٱللَّهِ

Who is better in speech than the one who calls to Allaah[2]

1 Soorah Fussilat (41):33

2 Soorah Fussilat (41):33

and remarked, "This person is the beloved to Allaah, the *walee* of Allaah, the elite of Allaah and is the most beloved to Him from amongst the people on earth. He answered the call of Allaah and invites the people to the very same call he responded to. He works righteous deeds within his response (to Allaah's call) and declares, 'Indeed I am from the Muslims...'"

There are many other Qur'aanic verses and *ahaadeeth* which mention the excellence of *da'wah* and the *daa'ees* (callers to Islaam). Likewise, there are many *ahaadeeth* concerning the dispatchment of *daa'ees* by the Prophet (ﷺ), which are well known to the scholars. From amongst these verses is this verse,

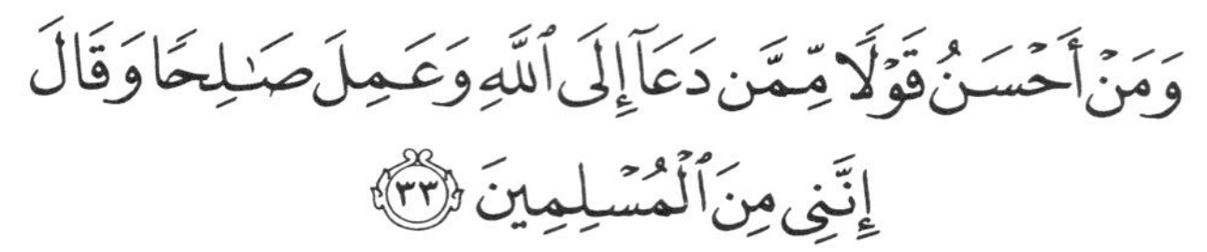

Who is better in speech than the one who calls to Allaah does righteous actions, and says indeed I am from the Muslims.[3]

This noble verse praises those people who give *da'wah* by stating that there is no-one better in speech than them. These *daa'ees* are headed by the Messengers, *'alayhimus- salaam*, and then those who follow them according to their rank in giving *da'wah*, in knowledge and excellence. So isn't it honourable enough for you, O slave of Allaah, to follow the Messengers and be from amongst those mentioned in this beautiful verse?!

So we have learnt that no-one is better in speech than the *daa'ee* because he calls people to Allaah, guides to Him and acts upon what he calls to.

---

3 Soorah Fussilat (41):33

The Prophet (ﷺ) said, "*Whoever directs someone to do good, he obtains the same reward as the one who does the good.*"[4]

This *hadeeth* is in *Saheeh Muslim* and tells us that the one who invites the people to do good and guides to it, has a similar reward to the one who actually does the good. Indeed it is a great virtue associated to *da'wah* and a great honour for the *daa'ees* (callers to Islaam) because Allaah, the Most High, gives the *daa'ees* a similar reward as He gives to the one whom He, the Most High, guides at their hands. What goodness, excellence and status it possesses! O my dear brother call to your Lord, your religion, obedience to your Prophet (ﷺ) and gain the same reward as the one who is guided at your hands, this is a great virtue and blessing.

Within this, is an encouragement and incitement for the *daa'ees* to give *da'wah* and to be patient upon it. If by these means you are able to obtain the same reward as the one whom Allaah guides at your hands, then it is more worthy for you to get qualified and to get prepared and hurry towards giving *da'wah* and be patient upon it, for there is great benefit in this.

The Prophet (ﷺ) said, as reported in *Saheeh Muslim* that "*Whoever calls to guidance, has the same reward as the person who follows him without his (the followers) reward being decreased one bit.*"[5] Indeed it is a great blessing that the one who calls to guidance obtains the same reward as the one who follows the guidance. This is similar to the previous *hadeeth* that "*whoever directs someone to do to good has the same reward as the who does the good.*"

---

4 Reported by Muslim [Eng. transl. 3/1050/no.4665].

5 Reported by Muslim [Eng/ transl. 4/1406/no.6470].

Furthermore one of the great favours of Allaah upon the male *daa'ee* is that he is a cause for the guidance of his father, mother, wife and offspring. Similarly one of great favours of Allaah upon the woman is her being a cause for the guidance of her husband, father, mother and her children. We learn this from the beautiful verse that the admission of the parents, spouses and children to Paradise with their relations is due to their righteousness.[6]

---

[6] The verse referred to here is:

جَنَّٰتُ عَدْنٍ يَدْخُلُونَهَا وَمَن صَلَحَ مِنْ ءَابَآئِهِمْ وَأَزْوَٰجِهِمْ وَذُرِّيَّٰتِهِمْ ۖ

Everlasting gardens of Paradise in which they shall enter, and (also) those who acted righteously from their fathers, their wives and their offspring...

[Soorah ar-Ra'd (13):23]

Chapter 2
The Ruling of *Da'wah* in General

As for its ruling, the evidences within the Qur'aan and *Sunnah* indicate the obligation of establishing *da'wah* to Allaah and that it is from the fundamental obligatory duties. Amongst the proofs are the sayings of Allaah, the Most High,

وَلْتَكُن مِّنكُمْ أُمَّةٌ يَدْعُونَ إِلَى ٱلْخَيْرِ وَيَأْمُرُونَ بِٱلْمَعْرُوفِ
وَيَنْهَوْنَ عَنِ ٱلْمُنكَرِ ۚ وَأُو۟لَـٰٓئِكَ هُمُ ٱلْمُفْلِحُونَ ﴿١٠٤﴾

Let there arise out of you a group of people inviting to all that is good, enjoining *al-Ma'roof* (the good) and forbidding the *al-Munkar* (evil), and it is they who are the successful ones.[7]

ٱدْعُ إِلَىٰ سَبِيلِ رَبِّكَ بِٱلْحِكْمَةِ
وَٱلْمَوْعِظَةِ ٱلْحَسَنَةِ ۖ وَجَـٰدِلْهُم بِٱلَّتِى هِىَ أَحْسَنُ ۚ

Call to the way of your Lord with wisdom and fair preaching and argue with them in a way that is better.[8]

وَٱدْعُ إِلَىٰ رَبِّكَ ۖ وَلَا تَكُونَنَّ مِنَ ٱلْمُشْرِكِينَ ﴿٨٧﴾

And call to your Lord and be not of those who commit *shirk*.[9]

---

7 Soorah Aal-'Imraan (3):104

8 Soorah an-Nahl (16):125

9 Soorah al-Qasas (28):87

Say (O Muhammad (ﷺ)) this is my way; I call to Allaah with sure knowledge, I and whosoever follows me (also must invite others to Allaah) with sure knowledge.[10]

Therefore Allaah, the Most High, clarifies that the followers of the Prophet (ﷺ) are those who call people to Allaah and are the people of insight, deep understanding (*baseerah*) and responsibility. When such a person hears something from the Prophet (ﷺ), he obeys him and follows his (ﷺ) methodology.

Allaah, the Most High, says in the Qur'aan,

لَّقَدْ كَانَ لَكُمْ فِي رَسُولِ ٱللَّهِ أُسْوَةٌ
حَسَنَةٌ لِّمَن كَانَ يَرْجُوا۟ ٱللَّهَ وَٱلْيَوْمَ ٱلْءَاخِرَ وَذَكَرَ ٱللَّهَ كَثِيرًا ﴿٢١﴾

Indeed in the Messenger of Allaah (ﷺ) you have a good example to follow for him who hopes in (meeting with) Allaah and the Last Day and remembers Allaah much.[11]

The scholars have explicitly stated that *da'wah* to Allaah is a collective obligatory duty (*fard kifaayah*) with respect to the regions where *daa'ees* are present, it is a collective obligatory duty. If a sufficient number establish the *da'wah* it is no longer held to be obligatory upon the rest. In the latter case it is regarded to be an emphasised *Sunnah* and an honourable righteous action.

---

10 Soorah Yoosuf (12):108

11 Soorah al-Ahzaab (33):21

If however, the people of a specific region or area do not establish the *da'wah* properly it will be held a sin upon each person and the responsibility has to be borne by everyone, each person giving *da'wah* according to his strength and capability.

With respect to countries in general, it is a must that a specific body be formed to carry out the *da'wah* to Allaah, the Mighty and Majestic, throughout the world, conveying the message of Allaah and explaining His orders through all possible means. For indeed, the Messenger (ﷺ) despatched *daa'ees*, sent letters to the people, Kings and leaders and called them to Allaah, the Mighty and Majestic.

Da'wah to Allaah is of two types: the first of the two is (*fard 'ayn*) an individual obligatory duty and the second is (*fard kifaayah*) a collective obligatory duty.[12]

It is *fard 'ayn* when no one is taking on the responsibilities such as enjoining the good and forbidding the evil. If you are in such a country, region or within a tribe and no one is giving *da'wah* to Allaah, commanding the good, forbidding the evil; if you have knowledge it becomes obligatory upon you specifically to give *da'wah*, guide the people towards the rights of Allaah, order the good, and forbid the evil. However, if there are present those who give *da'wah*, teach the people and guide them it will only be a *Sunnah* and not obligatory for others who also have knowledge of the *Sharee'ah*.

Likewise is the issue of *jihaad*, it is *fard kifaayah* when there is a sufficient number performing it. So *jihaad*, commanding the good,

---

[12] Translator's note: *Fard kifaayah* means 'a collective obligation' i.e., if it is fulfilled by a sufficient amount of people, then others are freed from the obligation. *Fard 'ayn* means 'an individual duty' i.e., obligatory on every individual.

forbidding the evil and *da'wah* are no longer obligatory upon the rest but an emphasised *Sunnah*. However, when there is an insufficient number, *jihaad*, enjoining the good and forbidding the evil becomes obligatory upon everyone.

Chapter 3.
The Ruling on *Da'wah* in this Age.

At a time when there is a shortage of *daa'ees*, when evil is prevalent and ignorance dominates (like our condition today), *da'wah* has become a *fard 'ayn* i.e., obligatory upon everyone according to their ability. If there is a confined area, like a village or a city etc., and there are some people who take charge of this matter and become involved in *da'wah*, and convey the order of Allaah; then this is sufficient and conveying the truth becomes a *Sunnah* for the rest of the people. This is because the truth has been established and the order of Allaah, the Most High, has been implemented by those people.

However with regards to the rest of the world and the rest of the people, it is obligatory upon the scholars and leaders - according to their abilities - to convey the message of Allaah in every way they can. Thus *da'wah* is a *fard 'ayn* upon them according to their strengths and capabilities.

In light of this, it can be seen that for *da'wah* to be *fard 'ayn* or *fard kifaayah* is a relative issue which varies. So it may be *fard 'ayn* with respect to certain groups and individuals and it may be a *Sunnah* to other groups and individuals because of the presence of a sufficient number of people who are establishing *da'wah* in their area.

In view of the spread of preaching towards destructive ideologies and atheism, denying (the existence of) the Lord, the Message, the Hereafter and the spread of Christian *da'wah* in many countries; in view of all this, establishing *da'wah* to Allaah, the Mighty and Majestic, today has become a general obligatory duty.

It is compulsory upon all the scholars and the rulers who profess Islaam, to convey the religion of Allaah according to their power and ability. They must call to Allaah, the Most High, through their writings, delivering public speeches, broadcasting, and through every possible way. They must not refrain from giving *da'wah,* or depend on others to give it.

The urgent need today, or rather the necessity, is for cooperation, participation and unification concerning this great matter more than ever before. This is because the enemies of Allaah have already united in solidarity and are cooperating with one another in every way they can to avert from the way of Allaah, put doubts in the religion of Allaah and call the people to that which will take them out of the religion of Allaah, the Most High. Therefore it is necessary for the people of Islaam (Muslims) to combat this heretical activity with Islamic activity and Islamic *da'wah* at all levels through all the possible means. This is enacting the duties of giving *da'wah* to Allaah which He has made obligatory upon us.

Today, we can see that the issue of *jihaad* has weakened, because the Muslims have undergone a change and split into many groups. Consequently the power and weapons have fallen into the hands of our enemy. Muslims today are only interested in their status, worldly desires and wealth, except those whom Allaah wills. And there is no movement, might or power except by Allaah, the Most High.

The only thing that remains in this age is conveying *da'wah* and guiding people to Islaam. Islaam has been spread in many places through *da'wah*; in East, West, and Central Africa, Europe, America, Japan and Korea as well as other countries throughout Asia. This is due to the *da'wah* which was spread partly due to travelling merchants (who took Islaam with them wherever they went) and through those who give *da'wah*, travel because of it and specialise in it.

Chapter 4.
The Aim of *Da'wah*

The aim of *da'wah* is to bring the people out of the darkness and into the light, and to guide them to the truth until they hold on to it and are saved from the Fire and the Anger of Allaah. To take the disbeliever out of the darkness of disbelief into the light and guidance, to take the ignorant out of the darkness of ignorance into the light of knowledge and to take the disobedient out from the darkness of disobedience into the light of obedience.

This is the aim of *da'wah* as Allaah says in the Qur'aan,

ٱللَّهُ وَلِيُّ ٱلَّذِينَ ءَامَنُوا۟ يُخْرِجُهُم مِّنَ ٱلظُّلُمَٰتِ إِلَى ٱلنُّورِ

Allaah is a *walee* (protector/guardian) of those who believe and brings them out of darkness into light.[13]

The Messengers were sent in order to bring the people out of the darkness into the light. Likewise the callers to the truth (*daa'ees*) establish *da'wah* and are active in it, in order to bring the people out of the darkness and into the light, rescue them from the Fire, obedience to the *shaytaan* and to save them from obeying their desires to obeying Allaah and His Messenger (ﷺ).

The aim of *da'wah* and *jihaad* is not to shed blood, take wealth or enslave women and children, these things happen incidentally but are not the aim. This only takes place when the disbelievers refrain from accepting the truth and persist in disbelief and refuse to be subdued and to pay the *jizya* (tax levied on free non Muslims living under Muslim rule) when it is requested from them. In this case, Allaah has prescribed the Muslims to kill them, take their wealth as

[13] Soorah al-Baqarah (2):257

booty and enslave their women and children. To use them as support towards obedience of Allaah and to make the law of Allaah known to them, and so that they can be rescued from the causes of the punishment and distress (of the Hell Fire). Also through this, the Muslims escape the plot and aggression of those who struggle against them, and the obstacles they place in the path towards spreading Islaam, so that it doesn't reach the hearts and nations.

There is no doubt that all this is from the greatest qualities and virtues of Islaam, which the people of justice and deep understanding and insight testify to whether they are its followers or its enemies. It is from the Mercy of Allaah, the Most Wise and the All-Knowing who made this religion a religion of mercy, kindness, justice and equality which is suitable for every time and place, and superior to every law and system.

Even if the minds of all mankind joined together to assist one another in producing something similar to Islaam or better than it, they would never be able to do this.

Exalted be the One who has legislated this religion, how Wise and Just of Him! How deep His knowledge is concerning the welfare of his slaves! How far is His teaching from foolishness and jest! How close is His teaching to intelligent and sound minds and the natural disposition of man (the *fiṯrah*).

Chapter 5.
The Urgent Need for *Da'wah*

It is well known to all those who have even the least amount of knowledge or understanding that the Islamic world today, indeed the whole world, is in a great need of clear Islamic *da'wah*. *Da'wah* which explains the reality of Islaam to the people and clarifies the Islamic rulings, its virtues as well as explaining the meaning of ***Laa ilaaha illallaah*** (none has the right to be worshipped except Allaah) and the meaning of the declaration of ***Muhammad ur-Rasoolullah*** (that Muhammad (ﷺ) is the Messenger of Allaah). Verily most of the creation have not understood these two declarations as they should. They have ascribed partners with Allaah and become distant from Him. For indeed these two declarations are, in essence, the roots of the religion, the basis of the faith and the foundation of Islaam, around which it revolves.

There is an urgent need for the Muslims today, and indeed for the whole world today to understand the *deen* of Allaah, be shown its goodness and clarify its truth and reality. I swear by Allaah, if the people and the whole world knew of its reality today, then they would surely enter the *deen* of Allaah in crowds as they entered it after Allaah made His Prophet (ﷺ) victorious in Makkah (at the conquest of Makkah).

The society is in serious need of reform, the Muslim, and the non-Muslim societies alike. However the Muslim society especially, has the most need to adhere to the correct methodology and undertake the ways and means by which its reformation will come about. They have to tread the path which the best person of this *Ummah* followed, the beloved of the Most Merciful, the best of His slaves; the great Prophet Muhammad (ﷺ).

For this reason it has been made clear to every student of knowledge that *da'wah* is from one of the most important issues, and that the *Ummah* has great need or rather necessity for it in every time and place. This is because *jihaad* is nonexistent in most of the world, and the people are in a great need for *daa'ees*, and those who give guidance and who are all upon the light of the Qur'aan and *Sunnah*. Therefore it is obligatory upon the people of knowledge, wherever they are, to convey the *da'wah* and to be patient with it. Furthermore, their call to Allaah and Islaam should be based on the Book of Allaah and the way of Messenger (ﷺ), and his Companions, *radiyallaahu 'anhum*, and the methodology of the Pious Predecessors.

Chapter 6.
If One Becomes Alienated and is Shunned, then he Should Work Harder in his *Da'wah*.

This condition is the confirmation of what our Prophet and Messenger (ﷺ) has told us in an authentic *hadeeth*, "*Islam began as something strange, and it will return as something strange, so give glad tidings to the strangers.*"[14] In another narration it was said, "*O Messenger of Allah, who are the strangers?" He* (ﷺ) *replied "those who are steadfast in righteousness at a time when the people become corrupt.*"[15] In another version he (ﷺ) said, "*those who correct what the people have corrupted of my sunnah.*" [16]

So this noble *hadeeth* makes it clear to the people of intellect that calling to the truth and refuting that which the people have introduced into the religion - at a time when Islaam is strange - is regarded to be from the reformation which the Prophet (ﷺ) encouraged and praised it's people for. This great *hadeeth* also makes clear to the readers, that it is obligatory upon the people of truth - when Islaam has become strange - to become more active in explaining the rulings of Islaam, giving *da'wah* and spreading its merits and virtues, and fighting against the vices. It is also necessary for them to be firm upon that until they become one of the righteous people at a time when corruption is prevalent, and they become one of those who correct the mischief when the people are active in it. Indeed Allaah is the Granter of success, Exalted be He.

---

14 Collected by Muslim.

15 At-Tahaawee in *al-Mushkil* (298/1).

16 At-Tirmidhee (2765) at-Tabaranee in *al-Kabeer* (16/17), al-Bazzaar (3287) and others.

Chapter 7.
The Effect of *Da'wah* in Spreading Islaam.

The truth has been spread through the correct Islamic *da'wah*, which in turn has been aided and supported by *jihaad* whenever anyone stood in its way. We have seen how the Muslims drove away the Romans from the area of Shaam,[16] seized the kingdom of Persia and Islaam was spread in Yemen, and other areas in the Arab peninsula. All this was due to the sincere *da'wah* and *jihaad* for the sake of Allaah, the Most High, and the obstacles were removed from the path of *da'wah*.

In view of this it is understood that the spread of Islaam was fundamentally achieved through *da'wah*. *Jihaad* with the sword was only used to save the truth and suppress corruption and mischief at a time when people opposed and obstructed the path of *da'wah*. Thus it was *jihaad* and *da'wah* together which helped to open the doors to victories. This is because most people do not respond to *da'wah* in itself, as its teachings oppose and contradicted their own desires and their love for indulging into the forbidden as well as their corrupt and oppressive leadership. Therefore *jihaad* came to stop these types of people, who had been a huge obstacle in the way of *da'wah* and remove them from their positions. Thus *jihaad* aids *da'wah*, realises it's objectives and assists the *daa'ees* to accomplish their duty.

From the time of Aadam, *'alayhis-salaam*, up until the revelation of the Torah, there were many Messengers calling to Allaah (giving *da'wah*) but there was no *jihaad*. So, Islaam spread through *da'wah*, proclamation and through the Books sent down from the Heavens.

---

16 Translator's note: This is the area presently known as Jordan, Syria, Palestine and Lebanon.

Thus, through the *da'wah* of the Prophets, *'alayhimus-salaam*, and through warning the people, the *deen* of Allaah was spread. This carried on from the time of Aadam, *'alayhis-salaam*, until the time of Moosa, *'alayhis-salaam*.

Indeed al-Islaam is the *deen* of Allaah, as He, the Most High, says in the Qur'aan,

> **Indeed the religion in the sight of Allaah is al-Islaam.**[17]

It is the religion of all the Messengers and nations as Allaah mentions stating Nooh, *'alayhis-salaam*.

> **And I am commanded to be among the Muslims.**[18]

---

[17] Soorah Aal-'Imraan (3):19

[18] Soorah an-Naml (27): 91

Chapter 8.
The Correct Methodology in Giving *Da'wah*.

Nothing will rectify the latter part of this *Ummah* except that which rectified it's former part; this is what the people of knowledge and faith have said. Amongst them is the well known Imaam Maalik bin Anas, the *imaam* of Medina in his time, and a well known jurist. He was one of the four *imaams* who made this statement. The people of knowledge during his time as well as after him, all agreed upon it and accepted it. "The end of this *Ummah* will not be corrected except by that which corrected its first part".

Meaning that, that which rectified the early generations of Muslims i.e. following the book of Allaah and the *Sunnah* of the noble Messenger (ﷺ), is what will rectify the generations after him until the Day of Resurrection.

Whoever wishes to reform the Islamic society or any other society in this world by using other means besides the ones used to rectify the first generations, then he is in manifest error and is far from the truth. As there is no other way besides the way of the early generations.

Indeed the way towards reforming the people and establishing them on the correct path is by following the path which our Prophet (ﷺ) and his Companions, *radiyallaahu 'anhum*, were upon and then those who have followed them in righteousness until this day. This path is the path of adhering to the great Qur'aan and the *Sunnah* of the Messenger of Allaah (ﷺ), calling the people to both of them and studying their laws; by spreading the Qur'aan and the *Sunnah* amongst the people, upon knowledge and deep understanding (*baseerah*), and by clarifying what these two sources of revelation teach us about the correct basic *'aqeedah.*

It is common knowledge that the ways in which the Islamic and non-Islamic societies can be reformed, are only through those which were employed by the leader of the Messengers, the seal of the Prophet's Muhammad (ﷺ). His noble Companions employed these ways, who were headed by the rightly guided Caliphs: Aboo Bakr as-Siddeeq, 'Umar al-Faarooq, 'Uthmaan Dhun-Nurayn, 'Alee ibn Abee Taalib Abul-Hasan al-Murtada and then those who were with them. May we become from amongst those who follow them in righteousness.

Every innovation, misguidance and methodology (*minhaaj*) that contradicts the law of Allaah, must be discarded. Everyone must follow the *minhaaj* (methodology) that the Messenger of Allaah (ﷺ) was upon in his life time, then his Companions, *radiyallaahu 'anhum*, after that, and the rightly guided Caliphs who followed him (ﷺ) and then the rightly guided *Imaams* and the righteous predecessors who followed them. They were all upon the correct methodology and the *siraat al-mustaqeem* (the straight path).

This is the methodology that everyone must take hold of and cling on to, be steadfast upon and call people towards, and anything which the people have introduced into the *deen* which contradicts this must be discarded and rejected.

Chapter 9.
Concentrating on Calling People to *Tawheed* (Singling out Allaah for Worship)

Verily the greatest and the most important issue that one should be concerned with is the issue of *'aqeedah*; the issue of *tawheed* and it's opposite.

Tawheed is the reason that Allaah, the Most High, sent the Messengers, revealed the Books, and created mankind and *jinn*. The other regulations in Islaam are all secondary to *tawheed*.

Allaah says in the Qur'aan,

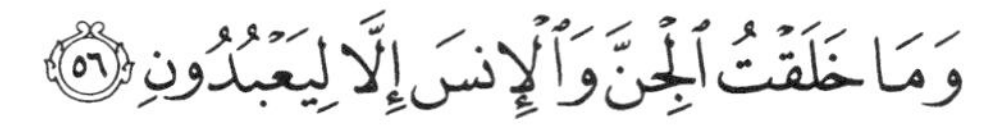

> **I have not created *jinn* and mankind except to worship me.**[19]

This basic foundation and greatest command is the first thing writers write about in their books. The *daa'ees* should concern themselves with this when giving guidance and aiding the truth. It is the truest science that one should cling on to with steadfastness and spread among all classes of people until they know its reality and distance themselves from that which contradicts it.

Indeed, I advice my brothers, the people of knowledge and those giving *da'wah* to concentrate on this great matter (i.e. *tawheed*), and write as much as they can about it in articles and letters; until (the knowledge of *tawheed*) is spread to the people and it becomes known to the elite and general public, as it is an issue of great importance and there is a urgent need for people to be aware of it.

---

[19] Soorah adh-Dhaariyaat (51):56

The first thing that the Prophet (ﷺ) did and the foundation that he laid was to call the people to the *tawheed* of Allaah and sincerity in worshipping Him, the Most High.

This is the first thing that one should do and the fundamental issue that one should talk about, invite others to and himself be upon, is *da'wah* (calling the people) to the *tawheed* of Allaah and guiding them to its explanation.

The statement that proves this is: *laa ilaaha illallaah* none has the right to be worshipped except Allaah. This is the firm foundation and with it is the declaration: *Muhammad ur-rasoolullah* Muhammad (ﷺ) is the Messenger of Allaah.

The proof for this understanding is strengthened by the fact that the Prophet lived in Makkah for ten years and called the people to the *tawheed* of Allaah, before prayer and other duties were obligated upon them. All of the Prophet's (ﷺ) *da'wah* was directed towards the *tawheed* of Allaah, leaving *shirk*, discarding idols and proclaiming the obligation upon all *jinn* and mankind to worship Allaah alone as well as leaving the *shirk* which their ancestors (i.e., of the pagan Arabs) and those who came before them were upon.

It is the ignorance of *tawheed* in most Islamic countries which has led people to their extremism of glorifying graves, especially the graves of those whom they call *awliyaa* or protectors and helpers. Mosques are built upon these graves and much worship is directed towards its people; acts of worship such as making supplications, calling for help, sacrificing animals, vowing and pledging etc.

It is also due to the ignorance of this fundamental issue of *tawheed*, that most Islamic countries rule according to man-made laws and ideas. They turn away from the rule of Allaah and His Messenger (ﷺ) which is the most just and perfect of all laws.

Chapter 10.
Comprehensive *Da'wah*.

The first thing that the *daa'ee* should call to and clarify to the people - just as the Prophet (ﷺ) had done so - is *da'wah* to the straight path of Allaah, which is al-Islaam, the *deen* of truth; and this should be the position that *da'wah* should have.

Allaah, the Most High, says in the Qur'aan,

Call to the way of your Lord[20]

The way of Allaah, the Mighty and Majestic, is submission, the straight path, the *deen* of Allaah which He sent His Messenger (ﷺ) with. Therefore, this is what you must call to, not to the *madhhab* of such and such person nor to the opinion of any individual. Rather you should call to the Religion, the straight path of Allaah upon which He sent His Messenger and the one He loves the Prophet Mu<u>h</u>ammad (ﷺ).

The way of Allaah is that which the noble Qur'aan and the pure established *Sunnah* of the Messenger (ﷺ) directs one to. The top priority of which is to call to the correct *'aqeedah*, sincerity towards Allaah and *taw<u>h</u>eed* in worship as well as *eemaan* in Allaah, His Messengers, the Last Day and everything which Allaah and His Messenger (ﷺ) have informed us about. This is the basis of the straight path.

It is the call to the declaration of *laa ilaaha illallaah* none has the right to be worshipped except Allaah and *Mu<u>h</u>ammad ur-Rasoolullah* Mu<u>h</u>ammad (ﷺ) is the Messenger of Allaah.

---

[20] Soorah an-Na<u>h</u>l (16):125

This means to give *da'wah* to the *tawheed* of Allaah, sincerity towards Him, belief in Him and His Messengers, *'alayhimus-salaam*, and including everything that He, the Most High, and His Messenger (ﷺ) has informed us about concerning issues of the Hereafter and the end of time etc. This also includes *da'wah* to what Allaah has enjoined, e.g. to make *jihaad* for the sake of Allaah, enjoining the good and forbidding the evil and accepting readily that which Allaah has prescribed regarding purification *(tahaarah),* prayer *(salaah),* mutual transactions/conduct *(mu'aamalaat),* marriage *(nikaah),* divorce *(talaaq),* (serious) crime, maintenance, war and peace and regarding everything because the *deen* (religion) of Allaah is a complete *deen* and it encompasses the welfare of the slaves in this life and the next. Islaam includes everything that the people need in relation to their religion.

The *deen* of Allaah calls to noble characteristics, good actions and forbids bad characteristics and evil actions.

The *deen* of Allaah is worship and leadership, because the Muslim is a worshipper and a leader of an army.

The *deen* of Allaah is worship and rule because the slave of Allaah worships, prays and fasts and he also rules by the law of Allaah, executing His orders.

The *deen* of Allaah is worship and *jihaad* because the slave invites the people to Allaah and fights in the way of Allaah, those people who leave His *deen.*

The *deen* of Allaah is (the) Book and sword because the slave of Allaah reflects and ponders over the Qur'aan and implements it's law by force, even with the sword if the need arises.

The *deen* of Allaah is politics and sociology because it calls to righteous and kind manners, brotherhood based on faith and unity of the Muslims.

As Allaah says in the Qur'aan,

> **And hold fast, all of you together to the rope of Allaah and be not divided among yourselves.**[21]

So the *deen* of Allaah calls to unity and upright and wise politics which unite the people and do not divide them, to the purity of the heart, respect for the Islamic brotherhood, cooperation upon piety and *taqwa* and guidance for the slaves of Allaah. The *deen* of Allaah also calls to enjoining trustworthiness i.e. giving back ones trust etc.

It is obligatory for the *daa'ees* to concentrate on refining and purifying the *'aqeedah* from superstition, innovation and *shirk* which has polluted it. And should undertake to spread Islaam based on all of its regulations and morals. This is achieved by making the people understand the Qur'aan and the *Sunnah*. The Qur'aan is the fundamental source for calling the people to good; then the *Sunnah* after that, which explains and elaborates on the Qur'aan. The *Sunnah* directs the people to the Qur'aan and clarifies and explains its meaning. And with regard to the character of the Prophet (ﷺ), the Muslims must take the Prophet as an example and model to follow.

To Summarise:

It is necessary for the Muslim *daa'ee* to call the people to the whole

---

[21] Soorah Aal-'Imraan (3):103

of Islaam and not to cause division among them, nor to be a blind follower of a *madhhab*, a tribe, to his Shaykh or to his leader etc. Rather his aim should be to affirm and clarify the truth and establish the people upon that truth, even if it contradicts the opinion of so and so or such and such person.

Chapter 11.
Patience of the Prophet (ﷺ) in Giving *Da'wah*.

Allaah, the Most High, has sealed the line of Messengers with the best of them, their leader and chief; Our Prophet and leader Muhammad ibn 'Abdullaah, may the peace and blessings of Allaah be upon them all.

He (ﷺ) conveyed the message, fulfilled his trust, advised the *Ummah* and struggled for the sake of Allaah, and he also fulfilled the right of *jihaad*. He (ﷺ) called the people to Allaah secretly and openly, and he (ﷺ) also endured great pain for the sake of Allaah.

However, despite this, he (ﷺ) remained patient in giving *da'wah* like the Messengers who came before him, *'alayhimus-salaam*. Like them, he (ﷺ) was patient and conveyed the message, however he (ﷺ) was afflicted with greater harm and therefore had to have more patience and bore all the burdens of the message perfectly.

The Prophet (ﷺ) conveyed the messages from Allaah, called people to Islaam and spread its regulations for twenty-three years. Thirteen of these years were spent in Makkah calling the people to Allaah in secret, he (ﷺ) then later began to call the people to the truth openly. Through the course of his *da'wah*, he (ﷺ) was afflicted with more harm, nevertheless he (ﷺ) remained patient upon his *da'wah* and bore the harm and insults of the people.

Even though they knew of his (ﷺ) truthfulness, trustworthiness, excellence, lineage and status; but the reason for their stance was desires, envy and opposition from the notables and ignorance and blind-following by the general public. So the notables denied, were haughty and envious and the general public blindly followed, and imitated. Thus, the Prophet (ﷺ) was harmed even more.

A proof which tell us that the notables had known the truth but were stubborn is the saying of Allaah, the Most High, in the Qur'aan,

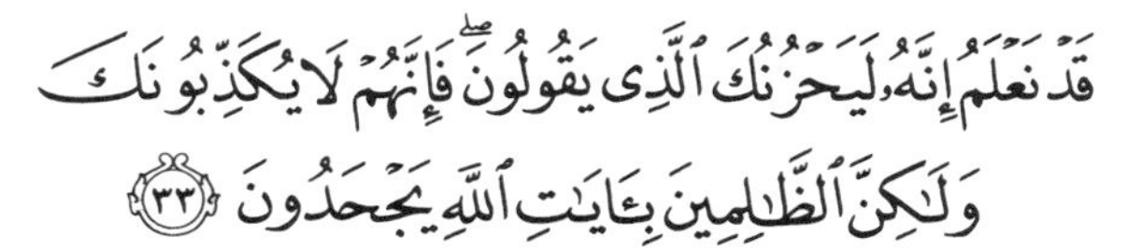

> **We know indeed the grief which their words cause you (O Muhammad (ﷺ)). Its not you that they deny, but it is the verses of Allaah that the *dhaalimeen* (wrongdoers) deny.**[22]

So Allaah explains that they didn't actually deny the Messenger of Allaah (ﷺ), rather they knew of his truthfulness and trustworthiness inwardly. They used to call him (ﷺ) "*al-Ameen*" (the trustworthy one), before he (ﷺ) was inspired by Allaah. However despite this fact, the people continued to deny the truth out of envy and injustice towards him. But this did not concern or worry the Prophet (ﷺ), and he (ﷺ) persevered in this path, remaining patient in anticipation of the reward in the Hereafter. He (ﷺ) continued calling the people to Allaah, the Most High, and patiently endured the harm. He (ﷺ) struggled with his *da'wah* and did not harm those who caused grievance to him (ﷺ).

The Prophet (ﷺ) tolerated and forgave everything directed towards him as much as he was able to until the situation intensified to the extent that his enemies decided to kill him (ﷺ). It was at this time that the Prophet was given permission by Allaah to migrate to Madeenah. So he (ﷺ) migrated.

Consequently, Madeenah became the first capital city of Islaam, where the religion emerged and the Muslims attained a State and

---

[22] Soorah al-An'aam (6):33

strength. In Madeenah, the Prophet (ﷺ) continued to give *da'wah* and clarifying the truth. He (ﷺ) legislated *jihaad* with the sword, sent Messengers calling the people to good and guidance, and explaining the *da'wah* of their Prophet to them.

The Messenger (ﷺ) also sent military forces and carried out well known military expeditions until Allaah granted His *deen* victory through him (ﷺ); and until He, the Most High, completed the *deen* and His favour upon the Messenger (ﷺ) and upon his *Ummah*. After Allaah perfected the religion through him and the Prophet (ﷺ) had clearly conveyed the message, he passed away.

Chapter 12. The Struggle of the Companions, *radiyallaahu 'anhum,* and the Pious Predecessors in Spreading Islaam.

After the Prophet (ﷺ) passed away, the Companions, *radiyallaahu 'anhum,* carried the responsibility and the trust of calling to Allaah and followed in the footsteps of the Prophet (ﷺ).

They called to Allaah and spread themselves all over the world, inviting the people to the truth, struggling and fighting for the sake of Allaah, the Most High, not fearing anyone except Allaah. They were spread across the world as military fighters, as rightly guided *daa'ees* to Islaam and as righteous reformers spreading the *deen* of Allaah.

The Companions and the *salaf* taught the law of Allaah to the people and clarified to them the *'aqeedah* which Allaah sent His Messengers with. Which was being sincere in worshipping Allaah alone and leaving the worship of others besides Him, the Most High, including trees, stones and idols amongst other things. So no one is to be invoked besides Allaah alone, no one's help is sought except Allaah's alone, no one's law is to be ruled by except His, no one is to be prayed to except Him, no one is to be made a vow to except Him, and other such acts of worship. The Companions also explained to the people that it is the right of Allaah to be worshipped and they recited the verses of the Qur'aan which mentioned this.

Allaah, the Most High, says,

يَٰٓأَيُّهَا ٱلنَّاسُ ٱعۡبُدُواْ رَبَّكُمُ

O people worship your Lord[23]

[23] Soorah al-Baqarah (2):21

وَقَضَىٰ رَبُّكَ أَلَّا تَعْبُدُوٓاْ إِلَّآ إِيَّاهُ

Your Lord has decreed that you worship none but Him[24]

إِيَّاكَ نَعْبُدُ وَإِيَّاكَ نَسْتَعِينُ ﴿٥﴾

You we worship and you we seek help from.[25]

فَلَا تَدْعُواْ مَعَ ٱللَّهِ أَحَدًا ﴿١٨﴾

Invoke not anyone with Allaah.[26]

قُلْ إِنَّ صَلَاتِي وَنُسُكِي وَمَحْيَايَ وَمَمَاتِي لِلَّهِ رَبِّ ٱلْعَٰلَمِينَ ﴿١٦٢﴾ لَا شَرِيكَ لَهُۥ وَبِذَٰلِكَ أُمِرْتُ وَأَنَا۠ أَوَّلُ ٱلْمُسْلِمِينَ

Say (O Muhammad (ﷺ)) "Verily my prayer, my sacrifice, my living and my dying are for Allaah, the Lord of the worlds. He has no partner. And of this I have been commanded, and I am the first of the Muslims"[27]

Furthermore the Companions, *radiyallaahu 'anhum,* had great patience upon this and they struggled immensely for the sake of Allaah. They, *radiyallaahu 'anhum,* were followed in this by the *imaams* of guidance from the *taabi'een* (the successors) and the *atbaa at-taabi'een* (their successors), Arab and non-Arab alike. They took this path, the path of *da'wah*, bearing its burden and fulfilling the

---

[24] Soorah al-Israa' (17):23

[25] Soorah al-Faatihah (1):5

[26] Soorah al-Jinn (72):18

[27] Soorah al-An'aam (6):162-3

trust with truthfulness, patience and sincerity in the struggle for the sake of Allaah. They fought those who left His, the Most High's, religion and those who obstructed others from His path and didn't pay the *jizya* (a tax levied for the non-Muslims living under Muslim rule) which Allaah has made obligatory upon some of the disbelievers. They are the carriers of the *da'wah* and the *imaams* of guidance after the Prophet (ﷺ), similar to them were the *taabi'een, itba'at-taabi'een* and the *imaams* of guidance who followed the *sahaabah, radiyallaahu 'anhum.*

Chapter 13.
The Reason for the Weakness of the Muslims and the Path Towards Restoring their Honour

When the people began to change and split up into groups and became negligent of the issue of *jihaad*, preferring ease and to follow their desires. Then, evil began to manifest itself in them, except in those people whom Allaah, the Most High, had safeguarded.

So as a result of this Allaah changed their position and gave their enemies power over them, an outcome which the people earned themselves and it is not an oppression from their Lord.

Allaah the Most High, says,

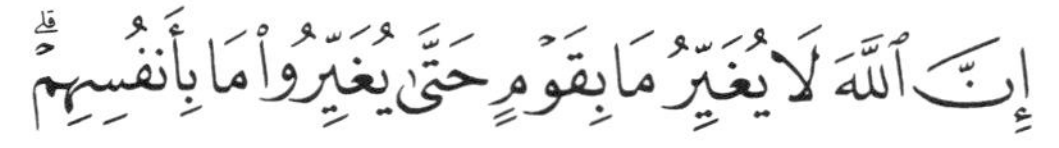

> **Indeed Allaah does not change the condition of a people until they change themselves.**[28]

Therefore it is necessary for all Muslims, governments and people to return to their Lord, the Most High, sincerely worshipping and repenting to Him for their shortcomings and the sins which they have committed. They should hurry to fulfil their obligations and distant themselves from that which Allaah has forbidden, and join with one another in co-operation in this.

From one of the most important of these issues is to establish the laws of the *Shar'eeah* and govern the people by it in everything, so that the people appeal to this *Shar'ee* law for legal decisions and not to the man-made laws which oppose the law of Allaah, which should be declared void.

---

[28] Soorah ar-Ra'd (13):11

In addition to this, the people should be made to adhere to the laws of the *Sharee'ah*, just as the scholars must teach the people their religion, spread Islamic education amongst them and urge each other to the truth and patience upon it as well as enjoin the good (*al-ma'roof*), forbid the evil (*al-munkar*) and encourage the rulers upon that.

Likewise it is necessary to struggle and fight against the destructive principles of socialism, the *ba'thiyyah* and national partisanship as well as other ideologies and schools of thought which lie in contradiction to the *Sharee'ah*.

If all the Muslims strive towards this, then consequently, Allaah will reform that which is corrupt and misguiding for the Muslims and restore them to their former glory and make them victorious over their enemies and powerful on earth.

As Allaah, the Most High, says, and He is the Most Truthful in speech,

وَكَانَ حَقًّا عَلَيْنَا نَصْرُ ٱلْمُؤْمِنِينَ ﴿٤٧﴾

It was incumbent upon Us to help the believers.[29]

وَعَدَ ٱللَّهُ ٱلَّذِينَ ءَامَنُوا۟ مِنكُمْ وَعَمِلُوا۟
ٱلصَّٰلِحَٰتِ لَيَسْتَخْلِفَنَّهُمْ فِى ٱلْأَرْضِ كَمَا ٱسْتَخْلَفَ
ٱلَّذِينَ مِن قَبْلِهِمْ وَلَيُمَكِّنَنَّ لَهُمْ دِينَهُمُ ٱلَّذِى ٱرْتَضَىٰ لَهُمْ
وَلَيُبَدِّلَنَّهُم مِّنۢ بَعْدِ خَوْفِهِمْ أَمْنًا ۚ يَعْبُدُونَنِى لَا يُشْرِكُونَ بِى
شَيْـًٔا ۚ وَمَن كَفَرَ بَعْدَ ذَٰلِكَ فَأُو۟لَٰٓئِكَ هُمُ ٱلْفَٰسِقُونَ ﴿٥٥﴾

---

[29] Soorah ar-Room (30):47

> **Allaah has promised those among you who believe and do righteous good deeds, that He will certainly grant them succession to (the present rulers) in the earth, as He granted it to those before them, and that He will grant them authority to practise their religion, that which He has chosen (i.e. Islaam). And He will surely give them in exchange a safe security after their fear, (provided) they (the believers) worship Me and do not associate anything (in worship) with Me. But whoever disbelieved after this, they are *faasiqoon* (rebellious and disobedient to Allaah).**[30]

Allaah, the Most High, also says in the Qur'aan,

إِنَّا لَنَنصُرُ رُسُلَنَا وَٱلَّذِينَ ءَامَنُواْ فِي ٱلۡحَيَوٰةِ ٱلدُّنۡيَا
وَيَوۡمَ يَقُومُ ٱلۡأَشۡهَٰدُ ﴿٥١﴾ يَوۡمَ لَا يَنفَعُ ٱلظَّٰلِمِينَ مَعۡذِرَتُهُمۡۖ
وَلَهُمُ ٱللَّعۡنَةُ وَلَهُمۡ سُوٓءُ ٱلدَّارِ ﴿٥٢﴾

> **Verily We will indeed make victorious our Messengers and those who believe in this world's life and on the Day when the witnesses will stand forth. The Day when their excuses will be of no profit to the *dhaalimoon* (polytheists, wrongdoers and disbelievers in the oneness of Allaah). Theirs will be the curse and theirs will be the evil abode.**[31]

The Muslims were only afflicted when they did not adhere to their religion as they should and when most of them do not understand

---

30 Soorah an-Noor (24): 55

31 Soorah Ghaafir (40):51/52

its reality. This is because the Muslims turned away from their religion, did not seek to understand it and the scholars fell short in explaining its virtues, bringing out its goodness, wisdoms and secrets, they were also deficient in their truthfulness and patience in giving *da'wah* and in enduring harm for its cause. As a result of this is the occurrence of the divisions, differences, ignorance of the majority with regard to the laws of Islaam and confusion of affairs witnessed in our present time.

Chapter 14.
Who is *Da'wah* Obligatory Upon?

Da'wah is an obligation upon everyone who has the ability, from the scholars to the Muslim rulers and the *daa'ees*, until the message of Islaam reaches all corners of the world in the different languages people use. This is the (type of) conveyance which Allaah has ordered.

Allaah, the Most High, said to His Prophet (ﷺ),

> **O Messenger proclaim (the message) which Allaah has sent down to you from your Lord.**[32]

Thus it was obligatory upon the Messenger (ﷺ) to deliver the message just as it was obligatory upon all the Messengers, peace and blessings of Allaah be upon all of them and upon those who follow the Messengers in conveying the message.

The Prophet (ﷺ) has said "*Convey from me even if it is an aayah.*"[33] And when the Prophet (ﷺ) addressed the people he (ﷺ) used to say, "*Let the one who is present convey what he has heard to the one who is absent, for the one who is absent may understand it better than the one who is present.*"[34]

Hence it is obligatory upon the whole of the *Ummah*, from the rulers, scholars to traders and others to convey this *deen* from Allaah

---

[32] Soorah al-Maa'idah (5):67

[33] *Saheeh al-Bukhaaree* [Eng. transl. 4/442/no.667].

[34] *Saheeh al-Bukhaaree.*

and His Messenger (ﷺ), and explain it to the people in the various languages which are used by them.

Chapter 15.
Da’wah Differs Depending Upon the Societies.

It is a fact that factors and societies differ. In a society which is waging war against the establishment of the *deen*, where there is no leader who helps you towards reform and guidance, then in this situation you should do as the Prophet (ﷺ) did in Makkah. You should call the people to Allaah in the best of ways, good manners and gentle words. So that what you say enters their hearts and influences them and so that the heart inclines towards obedience to Allaah and His *tawheed*. You should co-operate with your brothers and those who are upon your methodology to give *da’wah* and to guide the people through kind ways in societies where *da’wah* is allowed. This should be done until the faith is firmly established in the hearts of the people and Islaam spreads amongst the people with its clear proofs.

In an Islamic society, where there is an Islamic ruler who helps you, you must be more active in enjoining the good and forbidding the evil, communicating with the officials when there are people who stubbornly oppose Islaam and whose opposition is feared to be a danger upon society. In addition to this, you must follow the straight path with gentleness, wisdom and patience.

As Allaah says in the Qur’aan,

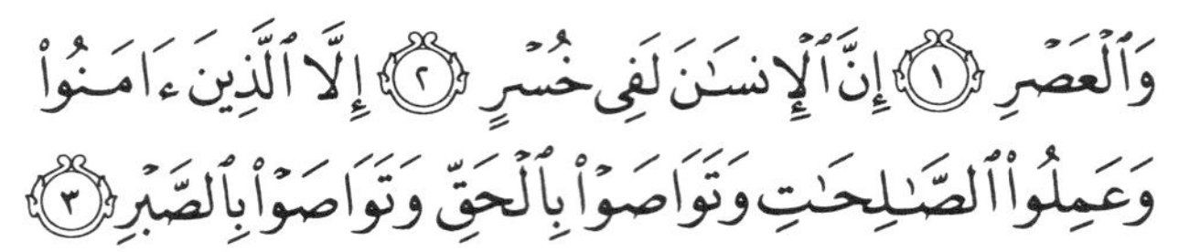

By the *’Asr* (the time), verily man is in loss except those who believe and do righteous good deeds, and recommend one another to the truth and recommend one another to patience.[36]

---

[35] Soorah al-’Asr (103):1-3

Chapter 16.
Who are the Saved Sect?

There are authentic *ahaadeeth* which have a similar meaning to the following *hadeeth*, in which the Prophet (ﷺ) said: *"All of my Ummah will enter paradise except he who refuses", it was said "O Messenger of Allaah! Who refuses (to enter Paradise)?" He (ﷺ) replied, "Whoever follows me enters Paradise and whoever disobeys me then he has refused (to enter Paradise)."*[36]

All of these *ahaadeeth* teach us that the saved sect from this *Ummah* are those who adhere to the *'aqeedah*, speech and actions of the Messenger of Allaah (ﷺ) and his Companions, *radiyallaahu 'anhum*.

Futhermore, the Noble Book of Allaah (ﷺ) indicates that which the *Sunnah* of His trustworthy Messenger (ﷺ) indicates i.e., that the saved sect are those people who follow the Book of Allaah, the *Sunnah* of His Messenger (ﷺ) and who are upon the methodology of His Companions with perfection.

Allaah says,

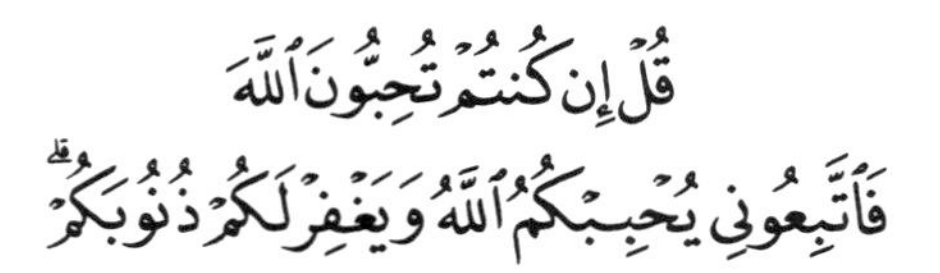

Say (O Muhammad (ﷺ)) "If you really love Allaah then follow me, Allaah will love you and forgive you your sins..."[37]

---

[36] *Saheeh al-Bukhaaree.*

[37] Soorah al-Maa'idah (3):31

وَٱلسَّٰبِقُونَ ٱلْأَوَّلُونَ مِنَ ٱلْمُهَٰجِرِينَ وَٱلْأَنصَارِ وَٱلَّذِينَ
ٱتَّبَعُوهُم بِإِحْسَٰنٍ رَّضِيَ ٱللَّهُ عَنْهُمْ وَرَضُوا۟ عَنْهُ وَأَعَدَّ
لَهُمْ جَنَّٰتٍ تَجْرِى تَحْتَهَا ٱلْأَنْهَٰرُ خَٰلِدِينَ فِيهَآ أَبَدًا ۚ
ذَٰلِكَ ٱلْفَوْزُ ٱلْعَظِيمُ ﴿١٠٠﴾

And the first to embrace Islaam of the *Muhaajiroon* (those who migrated from Makkah to al-Madeenah) and the *Ansaar* (the citizens of al-Madeenah who helped and gave aid to the *Muhaajiroon*) and those who followed them exactly. Allaah is pleased with them and they are well pleased with Him. He has prepared for them gardens under which rivers flow, to dwell therein forever. That is the supreme success.[38]

Hence, these two noble verses show that the evidence of ones love of Allaah is his following of the Messenger Muhammad (ﷺ) in belief, speech and action. As well as in following his Companions, *radiyallaahu 'anhum*, from the *Muhaajiroon* and the *Ansaar* and those who followed them exactly in belief, speech and action. These are the people of Paradise and dignity, they are the successful ones, Allaah is pleased with them and they are pleased with Him and they remain in the gardens forever. By the praise of Allaah this is clear and not hidden from the one who has the least amount of knowledge.

[38] Soorah at-Tawbah (9):100

Chapter 17.
The Way to Give *Da'wah* to Different Types of People.

There are many different types of people who are given *da'wah*.

The first type of people.

This type of person wants good but is negligent and has little insight and understanding *(baseerah)*. Therefore he needs to be given *da'wah* with wisdom this is achieved by making him understand the truth, guide him, and make him aware of the good in it in this life and the next. Then he will accept the *da'wah* and become aware of his negligence and ignorance, and will enter the truth.

The second type of people.

This type of person is one who is distant from the truth and occupies himself with other than the truth. Such a person needs good exhortation through *targheeb*[39]and *tarheeb*.[40] He also needs to be made aware that adhering to the truth embodies his betterment in this life and the next and that if he opposes the truth then he will be in distress, corruption and its evil consequences. Through this exhortation, he may respond to the truth and leave the falsehood he was upon. There is no doubt that this is a great responsibility which requires the *daa'ee* to have a high degree of patience, kindness, gentleness and understanding with the one he is calling. This is accomplished by imitating the *Imaam* of *da'wah,* our great Messenger Muhammad ibn 'Abdullaah (ﷺ).

---

[39] Translator's note: *Targheeb* is persuasion, i.e., when a person persuades another towards good by describing things of encouragement, e.g. Paradise, various rewards of good actions, the nature of Allaahs forgiveness and so forth.

[40] Translator's note: *Tarheeb* is dissuasion, i.e., when a person discourages another from evil by informing him of things which will discourage him from acting upon evil, e.g. the punishment in the grave, Hell-Fire etc.

The third type of people.

This type of person is one who has doubt, which obstructs his understanding of the truth and also obstructs him from obeying Allaah. Therefore, he requires the matter to be discussed and argued with him in a way that is best until he understands the truth and the doubt leaves him. Similarly the *daa'ee* must be more gentle and patient with him than with others in discussing and exterminating the roots of the doubt from his heart. This is accomplished by clarifying and explaining the different types of proof which clarify the truth, clearly and sufficiently in the language and customs of the one who is being called.

Since not everyone understands the Arabic language very well, even if he is from the people of knowledge, then the language, customs and traditions of his country may cause unclarity in the Arabic meaning intended by Allaah. Thereby he has made a great error by speaking of Allaah and His Messenger without knowledge. The consequences of this great corruption, in this world and the Hereafter are well known to the one who has the least amount of understanding.

In light of the above the *daa'ee* realises the urgent need to understand the *deen*, have a good understanding of the *Shar'eeah* regulations and know about the language and the customs of the people he is giving *da'wah* to. Thus it becomes necessary for the *daa'ee* to expand his understanding of the Qur'aan and the *Sunnah* and take care to know what Allaah and His Messenger intend. As well as to take care to study the Arabic language and the life of the Prophet (ﷺ), sufficiently, from the time that he (ﷺ) was sent by Allaah, the Most High, until he passed away. The *daa'ee* should study in this manner until he is able to guide the *Ummah* to the morals and the actions which the Qur'aan and the *Sunnah* of the Prophet (ﷺ) point out. Praise of this *daa'ee* will be in proportion to his *ijtihaad*, deeds and patience.

The fourth type of people.

These are the officials and notables whose evil one fears upon the *da'wah*. They should be advised with good manners, they should be guided and called through writing and through speech by the prominent men: the leaders and governors of the *Ummah*.

Allaah, the Most High, says in the Qur'aan,

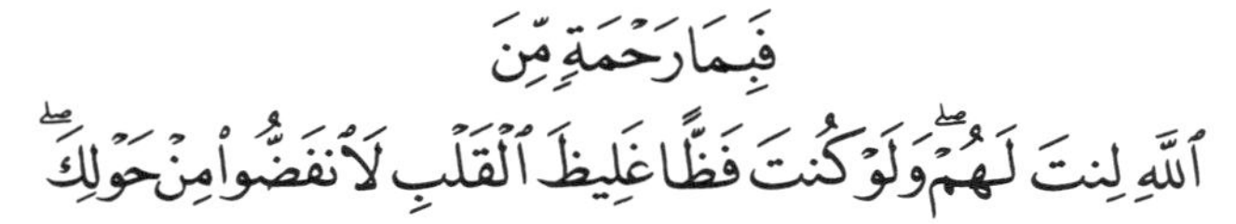

> **And by the Mercy of Allaah, you dealt with them gently. And had you been severe and harsh hearted, they would have broken away from about you.**[41]

Just as Allaah said to Moosa and Haaroon, when they were sent to the Pharaoh,

فَقُولَا لَهُۥ قَوْلًا لَّيِّنًا لَّعَلَّهُۥ يَتَذَكَّرُ أَوْ يَخْشَىٰ ﴿٤٤﴾

> **And speak to him mildly, perhaps he may accept admonition or fear Allaah.**[42]

The fifth type of people.

These are the disbelievers. You should call the disbeliever towards Allaah and make clear to him that he was created by Allaah to worship Him, the Most High, alone, and that it is obligatory upon him to enter Islaam and take that which the Messenger of guidance Muhammad (ﷺ) brought.

---

[41] Soorah Aal-Imraan (3):159

[42] Soorah Taa Haa (20):44

Chapter 18.
The Morals, Manners and Characteristics that a *Daa'ee* Should Possess.

The morals, manners and characteristics which a *daa'ee* should possess have been made very clear by Allaah in many verses of the Qur'aan.

1. Sincerity

The *daa'ee* must be sincere towards Allaah. He must not love to be seen and have vanity in his actions (*riyaa)*, or to perform an action whereby he desires others to talk about it and praise him for it (*sum'ah)*. Rather he should call to Allaah, the Most High, wanting to seek His Face alone.

Allaah says in the Qur'aan ,

قُلْ هَٰذِهِۦ سَبِيلِيٓ أَدْعُوٓا۟ إِلَى ٱللَّهِ

> **Say (O Muhammad) this is my way, I invite unto Allaah.** [43]

وَمَنْ أَحْسَنُ قَوْلًا مِّمَّن دَعَآ إِلَى ٱللَّهِ

> **And who is better in speech than he who calls men to Allaah.**[44]

So it is necessary to be sincere to Allaah. This is one of the most important morals and greatest characteristics that one must possess

[43] Soorah Yoosuf (12):108

[44] Soorah Fussilat (41):33

when one is calling to Allaah that you seek His Face alone and success in the Hereafter.

It is necessary that sincerity is towards Allaah and not to a *madhhab* nor to the opinion of this person, or that person. He must call to Allaah seeking His reward and His forgiveness and seeking the betterment of the people. Therefore it is necessary that he is sincere and knowledgeable.

Allaah says in Qur'aan,

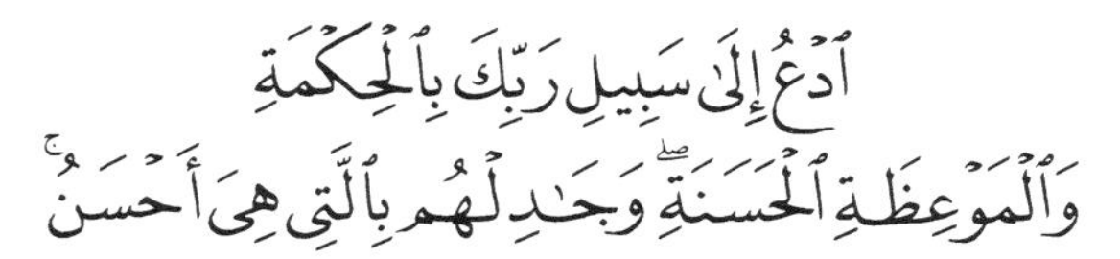

Invite (mankind O Muhammad (ﷺ)) to the way of your Lord with wisdom and fair preaching, and argue with them in a way that is better.[45]

2. Knowledge

You should give *da'wah* upon knowledge with clarity and not upon ignorance.

Allaah, the Most High, tells the Prophet (ﷺ), in the Qur'aan:

قُلْ هَٰذِهِۦ سَبِيلِىٓ أَدْعُوٓا۟ إِلَى ٱللَّهِ ۚ عَلَىٰ بَصِيرَةٍ

Say this is my way and invite unto Allaah with sure knowledge.[46]

---

[45] Soorah an-Nahl (16):125

[46] Soorah Yoosuf (12):108

Knowledge is therefore necessary as well as being a religious obligation. You must take care not to call while you are ignorant and you must beware not to talk about that which you have no knowledge of. The ignorant one destroys rather than builds, and he causes corruption rather than enjoining righteousness. So fear Allaah O servant of Allaah. Beware of talking of Allaah without knowledge. Only call to something after you have gained knowledge of it and a deep understanding *(baseerah)* about what Allaah and the Prophet Muhammad (ﷺ) have said concerning it. So it is necessary to have *baseerah* and that is knowledge. Therefore the student of knowledge and the *daa'ee* must reflect and pay attention about what they are calling to and its proofs.

If the truth becomes apparent and the *daa'ee* is sure of it he should call to that whether it involves doing something or leaving something. He should call to the action if it is in obedience to Allaah and His Messenger Muhammad (ﷺ) and he should call to abandoning that which Allaah and His Messenger Muhammad (ﷺ) forbade, upon clear proof and deep understanding (*baseerah).*

3. Kindness and understanding

Among the morals that you O *daa'ee* must posses is that you should be gentle, mild, forbearing, and patient in your *da'wah*, just as the Prophets were. Beware of being hasty, violent and harsh. You must have patience, understanding, and be gentle in your *da'wah*. Evidence for these qualities have already proceeded.

Like His saying,

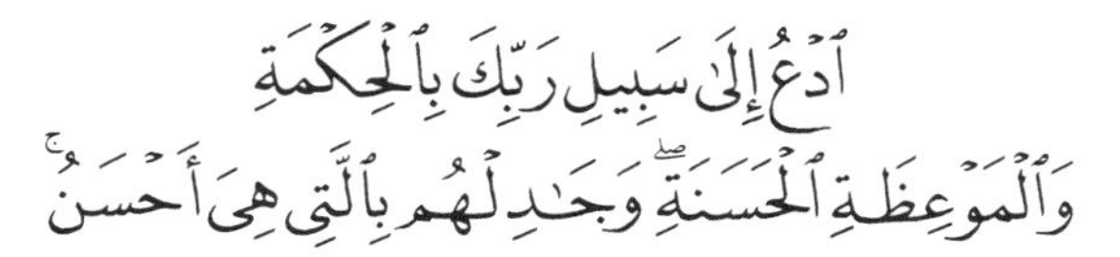

Invite to the way of your Lord with wisdom and fair preaching and argue with them in a way that is better.[47]

فَبِمَا رَحْمَةٍ مِّنَ ٱللَّهِ لِنتَ لَهُمْ

And by the Mercy of Allaah you dealt with them gently.[48]

فَقُولَا لَهُۥ قَوْلًا لَّيِّنًا لَّعَلَّهُۥ يَتَذَكَّرُ أَوْ يَخْشَىٰ ﴿٤٤﴾

And speak to him mildly perhaps he may accept admonition or fear Allaah.[49]

It has been reported in the *Saheeh* of Muslim that the Prophet Muhammad (ﷺ) said, "*O Allaah whoever acquires some kind of control over the affairs of my Ummah and is hard upon them, so be hard upon him, and whoever acquires some kind of control over the affairs of my Ummah, and is kind to them, so be kind to him.*"[50]
It is necessary, therefore, O servant of Allaah to be gentle in your *da'wah*. Do not make things difficult for the people, nor cause them to flee from the religion because of your harshness, ignorance and violent, offensive and harmful manner. You must be gentle, patient, soft and good in speech so that you affect the heart of your brother and the heart of the one you are calling to so that he likes to listen to

---

[47] Soorah an-Nahl (16):125

[48] Soorah Aal-Imraan (3):159

[49] Soorah Taa Haa (20):44

[50] *Saheeh Muslim* [Eng. transl.3/1016/no.4494].

your *da'wah* and he softens to it, is affected by it and he praises and thanks you for it.

As for violence, this leads to repulsion rather than drawing people close to Islaam and it causes division rather than unity.

Therefore gentleness is necessary when giving *da'wah* as the Prophet Mu<u>h</u>ammad said, "*Whenever gentleness is in something it does nothing but beautify it, and when it is removed from something it does nothing but disfigure it.*"[51]

The Prophet Mu<u>h</u>ammad (ﷺ) also said, "*The one who is deprived of gentleness, he is deprived of all good.*"[52]

So the Muslim must be gentle when giving *da'wah* and he must have a good manner in order to get a good response from the people rather than retaliation or rejection.

When should the *daa'ee* resort to harshness? We have seen that *da'wah* with harshness and force does much harm. What is necessary and more befitting for the *daa'ee* is to undertake *da'wah* by the means that Allaah has clarified in Soorah al-Na<u>h</u>l

Allaah, the Most High, says,

ٱدۡعُ إِلَىٰ سَبِيلِ رَبِّكَ بِٱلۡحِكۡمَةِ

Invite to the way of your Lord with wisdom.[53]

---

[51] *<u>S</u>a<u>h</u>eeh Muslim* [Eng. transl.4/1370/no.6274].

[52] *<u>S</u>a<u>h</u>eeh Muslim* [Eng. transl.4/1370/no.6270-6271].

[53] Soorah an-Na<u>h</u>l (16):125

However if the one you are calling is stubborn and oppressive, then nothing prevents you from speaking sternly to him.

Allaah, the Most High, says,

يَـٰٓأَيُّهَا ٱلنَّبِىُّ جَـٰهِدِ ٱلْكُفَّارَ وَٱلْمُنَـٰفِقِينَ وَٱغْلُظْ عَلَيْهِمْ ۚ

O Prophet (Muhammad (ﷺ)) strive hard against the disbelievers and the hypocrites and be severe against them.[54]

وَلَا تُجَـٰدِلُوٓا۟ أَهْلَ ٱلْكِتَـٰبِ إِلَّا بِٱلَّتِى هِىَ أَحْسَنُ إِلَّا
ٱلَّذِينَ ظَلَمُوا۟ مِنْهُمْ ۖ

And argue not with the people of the scripture unless it be in (a way) that is better, except with such of them as do wrong.[55]

The verses and *ahaadeeth* that have proceeded teach us that the complete Islamic *Shar'eeah* has told us when to use softness and when to use harshness. So the approach of the *daa'ee* must be characterised with softness, gentleness, and patience. This makes his *da'wah* more beneficial, influential and effective.

This is what Allaah has ordered and guided His Prophet (ﷺ) to do as well as to have sure knowledge and *baseerah* about what he is calling to and what he is forbidding.

Allaah says in the Qur'aan,

---

[54] Soorah at-Tahreem (66):9

[55] Soorah al-'Ankaboot (29):46

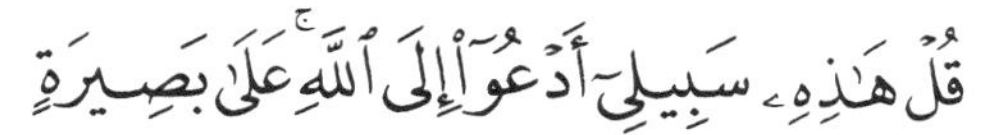

Say this is my way I invite unto Allaah with sure knowledge (*baseerah*). [56]

There is no need for the *daa'ee* to resort to being harsh or severe except when it is absolutely necessary and when he doesn't accomplish his aim by the first method (i.e., of using gentleness). Therefore the *daa'ee* acts justly in accordance to the situation and he employs the guidance of the *Shar'eeah* in both instances.

So it is required from those who call to Allaah, the Most High, and those who give advice to His servants to choose the beneficial methods and words which don't contain violence or deter people from the truth. Through this, the *daa'ee* hopes that it will make the one who opposes the truth to accept it and be pleased with it, preferring the truth and leaving the falsehood which he was upon. He should not in his *da'wah* use methods which deter people from the truth causing them to turn away from it and reject it.

4. Taking care to adhere to the Qur'aan and *Sunnah*.

Take great care to adhere to the noble Qur'aan through reciting it, reflecting upon it and acting upon it by following the pure *Sunnah*, as the *Sunnah* is the second source of Islaam and it explains the Qur'aan.

Allaah, the Most High, says in the Qur'aan,

[56] Soorah Yoosuf (12):108

بِٱلۡبَيِّنَٰتِ وَٱلزُّبُرِۗ وَأَنزَلۡنَآ إِلَيۡكَ
ٱلذِّكۡرَ لِتُبَيِّنَ لِلنَّاسِ مَا نُزِّلَ إِلَيۡهِمۡ وَلَعَلَّهُمۡ يَتَفَكَّرُونَ

And we have also sent down unto you (O Prophet Muhammad (ﷺ)) the reminder and the advice (the Qur'aan) that you may explain clearly to men what is sent down to them and that they may give thought.[57]

وَمَآ أَنزَلۡنَا عَلَيۡكَ ٱلۡكِتَٰبَ إِلَّا لِتُبَيِّنَ لَهُمُ
ٱلَّذِي ٱخۡتَلَفُواْ فِيهِ وَهُدٗى وَرَحۡمَةٗ لِّقَوۡمٖ يُؤۡمِنُونَ ٦٤

And we have not sent down the Qur'aan to you (O Prophet Muhammad (ﷺ)) except that you may explain clearly unto them those things in which they differ and as a guidance and a mercy for folk who believe. [58]

Real knowledge is what Allaah has said in the Qur'aan, and what the Prophet (ﷺ) has said in his authentic *Sunnah*. Therefore one should devote all his attention to the Qur'aan and the pure *Sunnah* in order to know what Allaah, the Most High, has ordered and what He has forbidden, so that he learns the methodology of the Prophet (ﷺ) in giving *da'wah* and forbidding the evil, as well as knowing the methodology of his Companions.

Therefore it is only proper for those with knowledge, the *daa'ees*, the teachers and the students all to devote their full attention to the Qur'aan so that they can be firmly established upon it so that it

---

[57] Soorah an-Nahl (16):44

[58] Soorah an-Nahl (16):64

forms for them a character and methodology which they traverse upon wherever they be.

Allaah, the Most High, says in the Qur'aan:

إِنَّ هَٰذَا ٱلْقُرْءَانَ يَهْدِى لِلَّتِى هِىَ أَقْوَمُ

Verily this Qur'aan guides to that which is most just and right.[59]

Allaah is the one who guides to the way that is most just and upright. Is there a greater aim for the believer than to be on this most just and upright way.

So it is necessary for all the people of knowledge and students to take care in adhering to what Allaah says and draw close to the Qur'aan through reading, reflecting, understanding and working in accordance with it.

Allaah, the Most High, says in the Qur'aan,

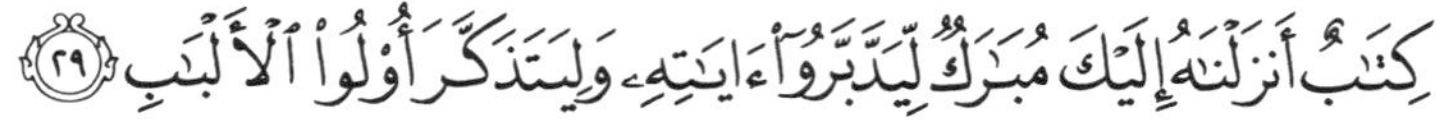

(This is) a Book which We have sent down to you, full of blessings that they may ponder over its blessings and that men of understanding may remember.[60]

The 'men of understanding' are those who Allaah has bestowed with sound intellect which enables them to distinguish between truth and falsehood and between guidance and misguidance. Whoever wants to acquire this great quality must devote himself to the Qur'aan by

---

[59] Soorah al-Israa' (17):9

[60] Soorah Saad (38):29

reciting it reflecting on it, understanding it and studying it with his colleagues. He must also question the people of knowledge about that which is difficult for him to understand and he should make use of the reliable books of *tafseer*, as well as adhere to the prophetic *Sunnah* because it explains the Qur'aan and directs to it. The *daa'ee* does this so that he can be firmly established on the straight path and is from amongst the people of the Book of Allaah, the Most High, reading, pondering and acting upon it.

5. Using wisdom when giving *da'wah*

Allaah, the Most High, says in the Qur'aan,

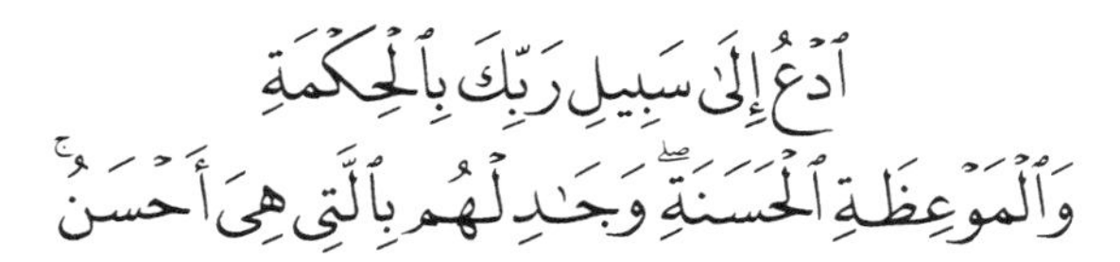

> **Invite to the way of your Lord with wisdom and fair preaching and argue with them in a way that is better.** [61]

Even though this is a glorious command which the Prophet Mu<u>h</u>ammad (ﷺ) was commanded to carry out, it is in fact an order which the whole *Ummah* must also carry out. Even if it is only addressing the Prophet Mu<u>h</u>ammad. He (ﷺ) is our guide and role model then it is a basic principle which is directed towards the whole of the *Ummah*. This is because the *Shar'eeah* states that the *Ummah* of the Prophet Mu<u>h</u>ammad (ﷺ) must follow him in what he has ordered and what he has forbidden, except when there is clear evidence that something was specifically ordained for the Prophet Mu<u>h</u>ammad (ﷺ). So, therefore *da'wah* is a religious duty and an obligation upon everyone.

---

[61] Soorah an-Na<u>h</u>l (16):125

Allaah, the Most High, says in the Qur'aan,

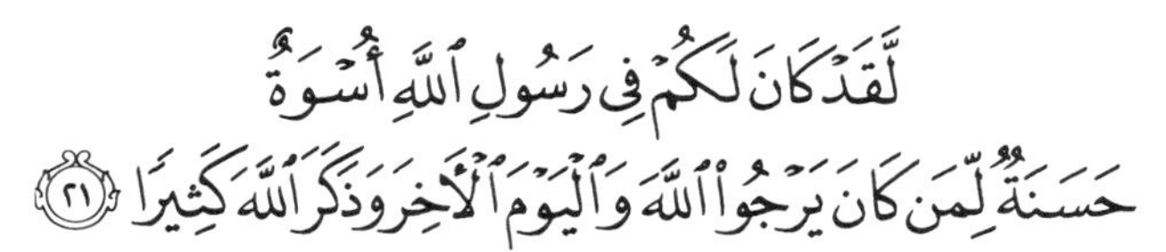

Indeed in the Messenger of Allaah you have a good example to follow, for him who hopes in Allaah and the Last Day (ﷺ) and remembers Allaah much.[62]

Therefore the Muslims should imitate the Prophet Muhammad (ﷺ) in giving *da'wah*, directing towards it and guiding the servants of Allaah to the causes of salvation and warning them against the causes of destruction. This great verse explains the manner in which *da'wah* should be given and the procedure which the *daa'ee* must adopt and what he should be upon.

Allaah, the Most High, says in the Qur'aan,

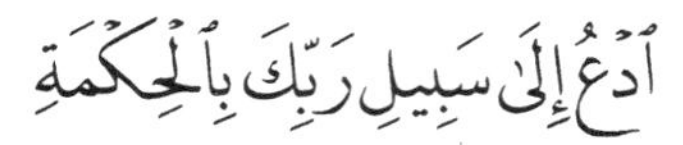

Invite to the way of your Lord with wisdom.[63]

Some scholars of *tafseer* explain that these verses mean: that one should give *da'wah* by using the verses of the Qur'aan and the *Sunnah* of the Prophet Muhammad (ﷺ): because of the wisdom that they contain and to the laws, prohibitions, explanations and the wise words which takes one away from falsehood and directs one towards good. Within it is the guidance and direction of the people towards that which holds happiness.

---

[62] Soorah al-Ahzaab (33):21

[63] Soorah an-Nahl (16):125

A part of wisdom is to clarify the meaning and explanation in effective ways. He does this in the language of the one whom he is calling so he can understand. The *daa'ee* continues in this way until the one whom he is calling has no doubt in his mind, and the truth which may have been hidden from him either due to lack of explanation or lack of persuasive *da'wah* in his own language, or because of unclarity in some of the proofs or an apparent contradiction of evidences, now becomes apparent to him.

Futhermore, If there is a need for religious admonition, then the *daa'ee* should preach and mention the suitable verses and *ahaadeeth* which concentrate on *targheeb* and *tarheeb*. The heart of the one who is being called will then awaken and be attracted to truth. So the *daa'ee* may need to use religious admonition *targheeb* and *tarheeb*, according to the situation of the one who he is calling to Islaam. Perhaps he is ready to accept the truth with the least amount of admonition because wisdom is sufficient for him. On the other hand he may be somewhat hesitant and reluctant. In this case he needs religious admonition and to be directed towards the remembrance of the verses which concentrate on *tarheeb*.

6. One must be a good example

Among the characteristics and morals which the *daa'ee* must posses is acting upon his own *da'wah*, and he must be a good example of what he is calling to. He shouldn't be someone who calls to something and then leaves that thing himself. Nor should he be someone who forbids an action and then does that action himself. This is the condition of the losers, and we seek refuge with Allaah from this.

As for the successful believers they call to the truth, act upon it, eagerly seek it, and hasten towards it. They also keep away from those things that they themselves forbid.

Allaah, the Most High, says in the Qur'aan,

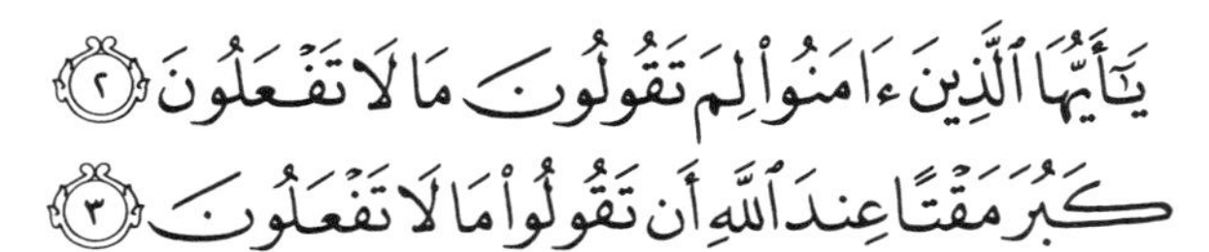

> **O you who believe! Why do you say that which you do not do. Most hateful it is with Allaah that you say that which you do not do.**[64]

> وَمَنْ أَحْسَنُ قَوْلًا مِّمَّن دَعَآ إِلَى ٱللَّهِ وَعَمِلَ صَٰلِحًا وَقَالَ
> إِنَّنِى مِنَ ٱلْمُسْلِمِينَ ﴿٣٣﴾

> **And who is better in speech than he who invites (men) to Allaah, the Most High, and does righteous deeds and says I am one of the Muslims.**[65]

This magnificent verse clarifies to us that the *daa'ee* must be one that acts righteously calling to Allaah, the Most High, with his tongue as well as with his actions as it is specified in the Qur'aan, وَعَمِلَ صَٰلِحًا **"...and (the one who) does righteous deeds."**

So the *daa'ee* must call the people with his tongue and with his actions, and there is no-one better in speech than these type of people. They are those who call and direct the people to Allaah through their pure speech, actions, and whole conduct which make them become righteous examples.

Similarly the Prophets, *'alayhimus-salaam*, gave *da'wah* through their speech as well as their actions and indeed through their whole way of life. Thus many of those who were being called, benefitted more from their conduct than from what they actually said, espe-

---

[64] Soorah as-Saff (61):2-3

[65] Soorah al-Fussilat (41):33

cially the general people and those deficient in knowledge. So these people derived benefit from this virtuous lifestyle, and their behaviour and their actions, to a greater extent then from mere speech which they may not necessarily have understood.

So truly the most important task for the *daa'ee* is that he must have a righteous lifestyle, he must be righteous in his actions and posses a righteous character so that he can be emulated in his words and actions.

7. To apply what he says

Allaah, the Most High, says in the Qur'aan,

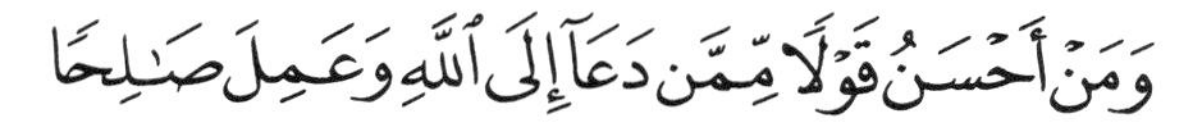

> **who is better in speech than he who invites (people) to Allaah and does righteous deeds.**[66]

This noble verse explains that the callers to Allaah are the best people in speech if they implement their speech by righteous actions and adhere to Islaam upon *eemaan*, with love and joy at this great blessing. As a result the people are influenced by their *da'wah*, benefit from it and so they love the *daa'ees* because of their *da'wah.*

This is contrary to those *daa'ees* who call to that which they do not do themselves. They do not receive any of this beautiful and sweet praise and nor does their *da'wah* influence or affect the community. Indeed, their only result in this *da'wah* is hate and disgust from Allaah, insults from the people, people turning away from their *da'wah* and warning others against it.

---

[66] Soorah al-Fussilat (41):33

Allaah, the Most High, says in the Qur'aan,

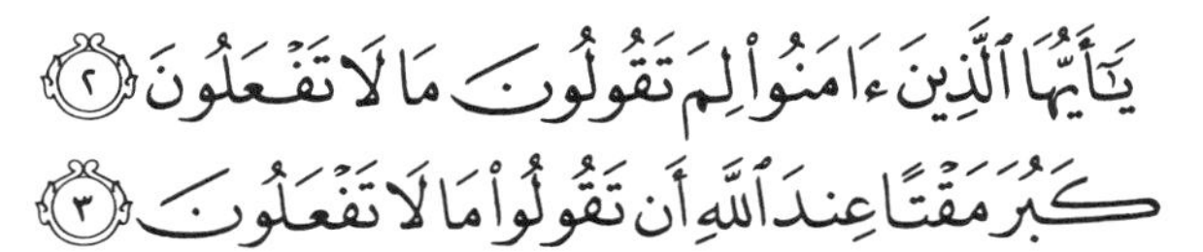

O you who believe why do you say that which you do not do. Most hateful it is with Allaah that you say that which you do not do.[67]

And He says when rebuking the Jews,

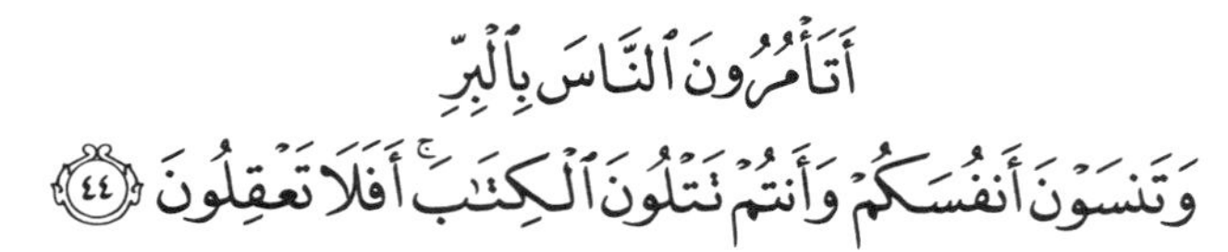

Enjoin you *al-Birr* (piety and righteousness and each and every act of obedience to Allaah, the Most High) on the people and you forget (to practise it) yourselves while you recite the Scripture, have you then no sense.[68]

So Allaah shows in this verse that the contradiction of the *daa'ees* action to what he preaches is illogical as well as being opposed to the *Sharee'ah*. So how can anyone who possesses any religion and understanding be pleased with such?

It has been authentically narrated from the Prophet Muhammad (ﷺ) that he said "*A man will be brought on the Day of Judgement and thrown into the Hell-Fire and his intestines will pour forth in Hell and he will go around them like a donkey goes around a millstone, then the people of the Hell-Fire will gather around him and they*

---

[67] Soorah as-Saff (61):2-3

[68] Soorah al-Baqarah (2):44

will say to him, 'Didn't you used to enjoin the good and forbid the evil?' and he will say, 'Yes indeed! I used to enjoin the good but I never practised it myself and I used to forbid the evil and I used to practise it myself.'"[69]

This is the state of the one who calls to Allaah, the Most High, orders the good and forbids the evil, and then his actions contradict his words and his words contradict his actions. We seek refuge with Allaah, the Most High, from that.

Amongst the most important and greatest characteristics with respect to the *daa'ee* is acting upon that which he calls to and desisting from what he forbids. He should have a righteous character, a praiseworthy lifestyle as well as being patient, persevering and sincere.

8. *Taqwa*

O servant of Allaah you are in serious need to have *taqwa* of your Lord. You should be firmly established upon it even in the presence of ordeals, or when you are afflicted with harm and mockery from the enemies of Allaah, the sinful and evil doers, do not let this worry you. Remember the Messengers, *'alayhimus-salaam*, and the ones who followed them in righteousness. They too endured many hardships and were mocked at and ridiculed by the enemies of Allaah but they were patient and their outcome in this world and in the Hereafter, was praiseworthy.

9. Being active and pleased in giving *da'wah*.

The believing *daa'ee* who is strong in faith, has a deep understanding about what Allaah has ordered. He declares the right of Allaah,

---

[69] Agreed upon, from the *hadeeth* of Usaamah ibn Zayd reported by Muslim [Eng. transl.4/1539/no.7122].

and he is active in giving *da'wah*. He acts upon that which he calls to and he is careful to stay away from that which he forbids.

He is the quickest towards that which he calls to and the furthest removed from that which he forbids. He clearly states that he is a Muslim and that he invites to Islaam and he rejoices and is delighted with that.

Allaah says in the Qur'aan,

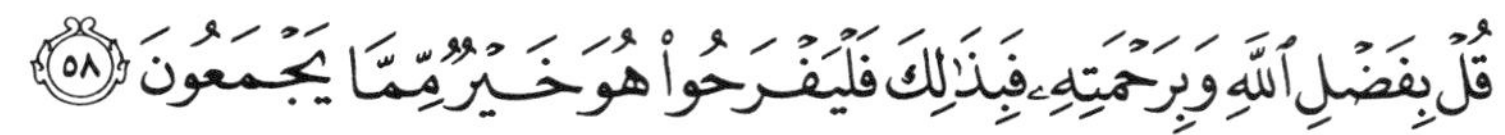

> **In the bounty of Allaah and in His Mercy therein let them rejoice. That is better than what (wealth) they amass.** [70]

So rejoicing in the mercy of Allaah, the Most High, is something which is allowed in Islaam.[71]

10. Supplicating for guidance of those whom you are calling

From among the righteous characteristics that a *daa'ee* should possess is that he should supplicate to Allaah to guide those whom he is calling, and say to them "may Allaah, the Most High, guide you and make you successful in accepting the truth." "May Allaah assist you with guidance."

When it was said to the Prophet (ﷺ) that the people of Daws had disobeyed, he said "*O Allaah give guidance to the people of Daws*

[70] Soorah Yoonus (10):58

[71] Translator's note: The reason for mentioning that "rejoicing in the mercy of Allaah is allowed", is to make a distinction between rejoicing sincerely and rejoicing in arrogance i.e., when a person becomes arrogant and proud when Allaah bestows mercy upon him. Therefore the Shaykh is saying that it is only rejoicing without arrogance, which is allowed.

and let them embrace Islaam."[72] So supplicate for the one you are giving *da'wah* to, to be guided and to succeed in accepting the truth, and be patient and persevere in that, and do not despair and become disheartened, speak only that which is good and do not be violent or speak badly by using foul and evil language, and thereby causing the people to avert from the truth.

As for the one who oppresses and shows aggression then his is another matter as Allaah, the Most High, says in the Qur'aan,

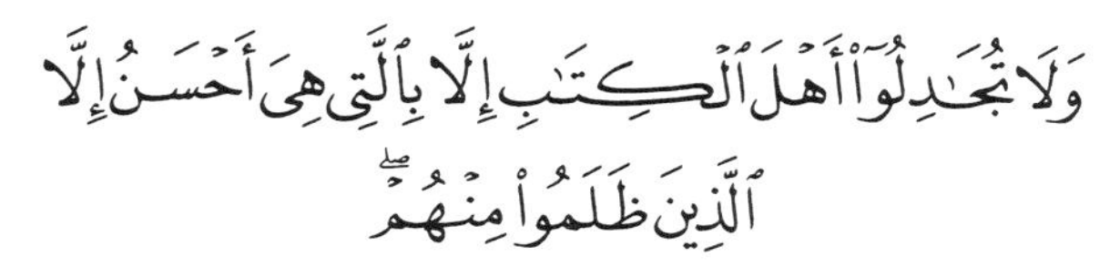

> **And argue not with the people of the scripture unless it be in a way that is better except with such of them as do wrong.**[73]

11. Do not feel embarrassed or shy to give *da'wah*

The *daa'ee* should call the people to the truth and act upon it himself as well as forbidding the falsehood and warning people to stay away from that and he himself abstains from it and he should not be embarrassed to declare his beliefs. Rather he should say: "Indeed, I am a Muslim, satisfied and delighted with what Allaah, the Most High, has blessed me with." He shouldn't be like the one who is ashamed and hates to mention that he is a Muslim or that he is inviting people to Islaam, for the sake of honouring or flattering someone. And there is no movement nor power except with Allaah, the Most High.

---

[72] Agreed upon, from the *hadeeth* of Aboo Hurayrah, *Saheeh al-Bukhaaree* [Eng. transl.4/115/no.188].

[73] Soorah al-'Ankaboot (29):46

12. Following the truth

You must accept the truth and follow it when the proof is clear even if it means that it is contrary to a certain person's view. You must not blindly follow anyone, rather you should know about the excellence, virtues and values of all the *Imaams*. You should also be careful to protect yourself and your religion and take hold of the truth and be pleased with it, and guide others to it if you are asked. Fear Allaah, be aware of Him, be just to yourself with the belief that the truth is one. And know that if the *mujtahids* (scholars) give a correct ruling then they have two rewards and if they make an error then they have one reward, as it has been authentically reported from the Prophet Mu<u>h</u>ammad (ﷺ).

13. Giving mutual advice and being patient when enduring harm.

The *daa'ee* should advise and enjoin his brothers and his friends as well as the prominent people and the leaders in the community upon the truth with sincerity. You should deal patiently with any harm that may befall you from these prominent people or others in accordance with what is being conveyed in the following *soorah*,

Allaah, the Most High, says in the Qur'aan,

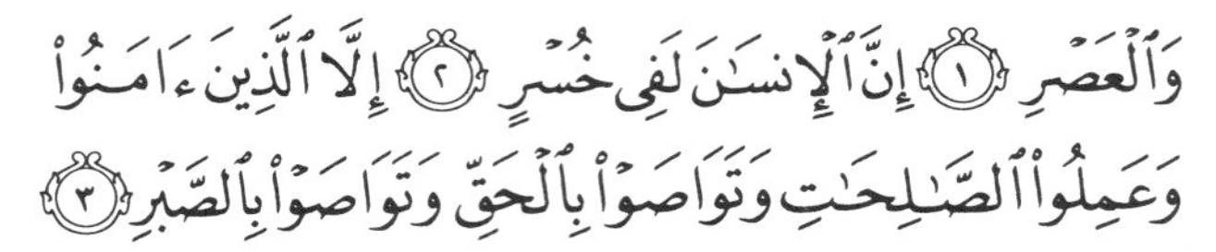

By *al-'A<u>s</u>r* (the time). Verily! man is in loss, except those who believe and do righteous good deeds and recommend one another to the truth and recommend one another to patience.[74]

---

[74] Soorah al-'A<u>s</u>r (103):1-3

Also in accordance with the noble Messengers as Allaah, the Most High, tells his Prophet Muhammad (ﷺ) at the end of the Makkan *Soorah al-Ahqaaf.*

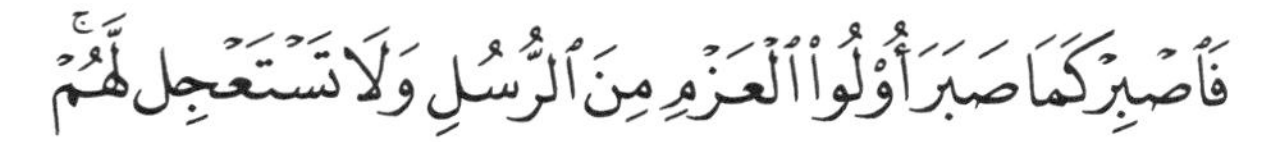

Therefore be patient (Muhammad (ﷺ)) as did the Messengers of strong will and be in no haste about them.[75]

14. Start with the most important thing and then the next in importance.

Those who guide others are the doctors of society. The doctor is interested in finding out the illnesses, then he works on their treatments by beginning with the most important of them. This was the method of the most sincere of doctors of the society, the most knowledgeable of Allaah and the most upright in fulfilling the rights of Allaah and the rights of His servants. He is the leader of the children of Aadam, the Messenger (ﷺ) .

Thus, we see that when the Prophet (ﷺ) was sent by Allaah, he began by forbidding the greatest illness: *Shirk* (associating partners with Allaah). From the time that he (ﷺ) was sent by Allaah and for the next ten years he never ceased to warn the people to stay away from *shirk* and called them to *tawheed*. After this he (ﷺ) then ordered them to pray and to abide by the remaining laws. Similarly the *daa'ees* after him must follow the same path and methodology employed by the Messenger (ﷺ), beginning their *da'wah* with the most important issue (*tawheed*).

---

[75] Soorah al-Ahqaaf (46):35

However, if the *daa'ee* is giving *da'wah* to a society of Muslims then it is permissible for him to begin by giving *da'wah* concerning other obligations alongside this most important issue of *tawheed*. Rather he must do this according to his ability.

Because the aim of *da'wah* is to reform the Muslim society and to exert ones efforts to purify the *'aqeedah* (beliefs) of the people from the evil of *shirk* and its channels, and to purify their characteristics from what weakens their *eemaan* (faith) and therefore harms the society.

If in some cases, the *daa'ee* does not find it easy to begin with this most important issue of *tawheed* then there is no harm in beginning with other issues. Nor is there any harm if he occupies himself solely with the most important issue (of *tawheed*), and pays very little attention to anything else if he see's the benefit in that and fears that if he were to engage himself with more than that then he would be unsuccessful in everything.

This is the methodology that the prominent reformers and doctors employ; they are concerned with the paths of reform and adopt the one most beneficial and closest to the desired result.

Whoever reflects on and looks attentively into the principles of the *Shar'eeah*, the life of the Prophet, the lives of the rightly guided successors and also the righteous *imaams* will understand what I have been saying and know how to set about and curing the people from their illnesses and guiding them to the place of safety.

Whosoever purifies his intentions; exerts his efforts to search for the truth, asks his Lord the Most Beneficial to guide him to the best path and to enable him to give *da'wah*; consults the people of knowledge and experience in matters in which he doesn't understand because they are unclear to him if he does all this, then he will succeed with satisfaction and happiness and will be guided to the truth.

As Allaah says,

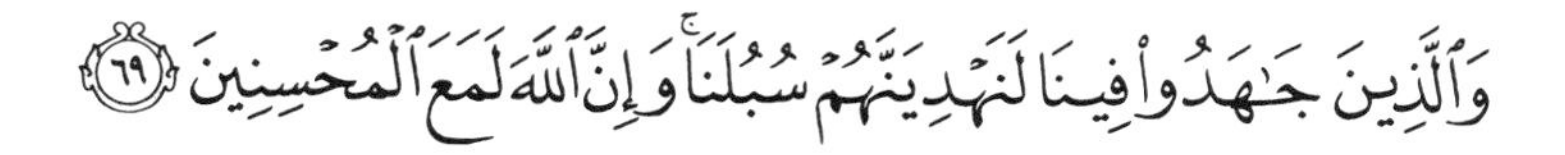

As for those who strive hard in Us (our cause), we will surely guide them to our path and verily Allaah is with the *muhsinoon* (good doers)[76]

15. Certainty in matters.

One should verify matters (concerning the religion) and give thorough consideration when judging them. This should only be done after studying them from all angles, ascertaining their meaning and having knowledge of their meaning based on the legal scales; which is the Book of Allaah, the Most High, and that which is authentic from the *Sunnah*. So accept that which agrees with the legal scales and leave that which contradicts it.

When the reader studies things according to the legal scales mentioned, he must distance himself from being excessive or deficient in what is required from him. He must also keep away from any type of partisanship and anything related to tribalism and his own whims and desires.

---

[76] Soorah al-'Ankaboot (29):69

Chapter 19
Asking the Scholars and Valuing Them.

Whoever is ignorant of the truth, he must ask the people of knowledge, i.e., those people who are known for their knowledge, their virtues and excellence, and the superiority of their faith and lives. He should look at them in this light, valuing the scholars, knowing about their excellence and virtues and supplicate for them to gain the highest degree of success and the greatest reward. This is because they have preceded us in reaching the great merits, virtues and goodness. It is they who taught, guided and made the path clear for us may Allaah, the Most High, have mercy on all of them.

It is the scholars who posses the virtues and excellence of preceding us, and the virtues of knowledge and *da'wah* from amongst the *sahaabah* and the people of knowledge, and *Imaams* that came after them. So one should know the magnificent value of these scholars. It is therefore necessary that we should seek Allaah's mercy upon them and follow them in our activities, in gaining knowledge in giving *da'wah* and we should always give precedence to what Allaah and his Messenger (ﷺ) have said.

One should be patient upon this, hurry to do righteous deeds and imitate the scholars in these great virtues. Seeking Allaah's mercy upon them.

However, by no means should one be inclined to one scholar completely, saying that he is always completely correct. Rather he should know that everyone can err (when giving a ruling) or he could be correct. The correct ruling is that which is in accordance with what Allaah and the Prophet Muhammad (ﷺ) have said, which has been derived from the Qur'aan and the *Sunnah*, through consensus of the people of knowledge. If they differ among themselves then they must all refer back to Allaah, the Most High, and the *Sunnah* of the Prophet Mu*h*ammad (ﷺ).

As Allaah says in the Qur'aan,

فَإِن تَنَٰزَعۡتُمۡ فِي شَيۡءٖ فَرُدُّوهُ إِلَى ٱللَّهِ وَٱلرَّسُولِ

And if they differ in anything amongst yourselves, refer it to Allaah and His Messenger.[77]

وَمَا ٱخۡتَلَفۡتُمۡ فِيهِ مِن شَيۡءٖ فَحُكۡمُهُۥٓ إِلَى ٱللَّهِۚ

And in whatsoever you differ, the decision thereof is with Allaah.[78]

And this is what the scholars of old and the present time have said.

---

77 Soorah an-Nisaa' (4):59

78 Soorah ash-Shooraa (42):10

Chapter 20
Using the Media for Giving *Da'wah*

The use of media has become one of the most successful and beneficial means of communication in this age. This is due to its popularity and it being a weapon with two edges.

If the media, such as radio, newspapers and television, are used for giving *da'wah*, and for guiding people to Allaah and what the Prophet Muhammad has brought, then this is a great thing which can benefit the *Ummah* wherever they are, by the permission of Allaah. This can also benefit the non-Muslims in helping them to understand Islaam and comprehend it, learn about its merits and know that it is the path to success in this world and in the Hereafter.

It is obligatory for the *daa'ees*, as well as for the Muslim rulers to contribute in giving *da'wah* in every way they can, through the use of radio, newspapers, television and in speeches given in gatherings on *Jum'ah* (Friday) as well as on other days. They should also use other means which enable the people to hear the truth, in all the languages used by the people, so that *da'wah* and advice can reach them wherever they are in the world, in their own languages.

Chapter 21
The Hastiness of the Youth and their Need for the Wisdom of the Old

The youth in any nation are the backbone which form the element of movement and vitality in society. They have the energy to bring about effective results.

Usually a nation is never revived except due to the awareness and continuous enthusiasm of the youth. However over enthusiasm of the youth must be guided through the wisdom of the old. The youth must contemplate and look into the experiences of the old, they shouldn't leave one for the other, but rather must preserve both of these qualities (the enthusiasm of the youth and the wisdom of the older generation). The *Ummah* is an *Ummah* with an eternal message and has supremacy over the other nations. When Allaah blessed this *Ummah* with this religion and with the sending of the leader of the Messengers (ﷺ). So the youth held an important role in propagating this noble and blessed *da'wah* just as the old had an important role in directing and supporting this *da'wah*. The young and the old both helped in establishing the first Islamic State, under the leadership of the Prophet Mu<u>h</u>ammad (ﷺ) which stretched to the furthest horizons, placing the banner of Islaam over most of the world.

Throughout the different ages of Islaam the youth were at the forefront, defending Islaam and protecting the Muslim areas with their tongue, hand, knowledge and action.

Chapter 22
When Should the *Daa'ee* Disassociate Himself From the Disobedient

This issue requires elaboration; it is permissible to renounce and disassociate from the one who makes public his evil and is insistent on this, and the advice given to him does not benefit him. It is therefore allowed for his relative or neighbour to boycott him by disassociating themselves from this person by not responding to his invitation (to dinner etc.) or giving him *salaam*. This is done until he returns to Allaah in repentance from this evil.

This was the case when the Prophet Muhammad (ﷺ) and his Companions disassociated themselves from Ka'b Ibn Maalik[79] and his two companions when they stayed behind during the Tabook expedition without excuse or legal reason. Thus the Prophet ordered the people not to speak to them and to keep away from them i.e. to boycott them. So the three of them were boycotted until they repented to Allaah, and Allaah accepted their repentance.

However in some cases, if a person is boycotted, it may lead to a greater evil than what he actually did because he may be a prominent and important person in the *Ummah* or in his tribe. In such a case the *daa'ee* should not boycott him but should deal with him in a way that is best. He should treat him in a friendly and gentle manner because boycotting him may lead to that which is more evil than his evil and what is more disgraceful than what he has done. The evidence for this is that the Prophet Muhammad (ﷺ) did not deal with the head of the hypocrites, 'Abdullaah ibn Abee ibn Salool, in the same way that he dealt with Ka'b and his two companions.

---

79 *Saheeh Muslim* [Eng. transl.4/1445/no.6670].

Rather he was kind to him and did not boycott him. This is because he was the leader of his people and the Prophet (ﷺ) feared the *fitnah* would spread amongst the whole of the city if he was boycotted and imprisoned. So the Prophet dealt with him kindly and on good terms, until he died on his hypocrisy.

The Prophet also dealt with other people in different situations. They too were not boycotted but were treated kindly until Allaah guided them.

So the issue of kindness when giving *da'wah* is one of it's most necessary features. And with Allaah is the success.

Chapter 23
Warnings to the *Daa'ee*

1. Beware of being extreme

It is correct to name this awakening which pleases and excites every believer, an Islamic movement, an Islamic revival and an Islamic activity. It is necessary to encourage and guide this awakening towards adhereing and clinging to the Qur'aan and the *Sunnah* of the Prophet Mu_h_ammad (ﷺ) as well as warning leaders and individuals within this awakening from exceeding the limits, exaggerating and being extreme in their actions.

In accordance with what Allaah says in the Qur'aan,

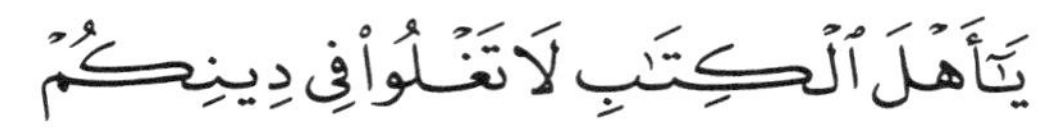

> **O people of the scripture, do not exceed the limits in your religion.**[80]

The Prophet Mu_h_ammad (ﷺ) is reported to have said: "*O you people, beware of being extreme and exceeding the limits in the religion, for that which destroyed the people before you was none other than extremism in the religion.*" He (ﷺ) also said: "*The extremists are destroyed, the extremists are destroyed, the extremists are destroyed.*"

2. Speaking about Allaah without knowledge

Beware of speaking about Allaah, the Most High, without knowledge. It is not permissible for one who believes in Allaah, the Most

---

80 Soorah an-Nisaa' (4):171

High, and the Last Day to say: 'This is *halaal* and this is *haraam*' or 'This is permissible and this is prohibited', except with a proof and completely depending upon that. It should be sufficient for him to do what the people of knowledge did before him, and that is to restrain oneself from rushing into saying that which he does not know but rather to say: "Allaah knows best" or "I do not know".

How excellent is the speech of the angels when they said to their Lord,

سُبْحَٰنَكَ لَا عِلْمَ لَنَآ إِلَّا مَا عَلَّمْتَنَآ

> **Glory be to You, we have no knowledge except that which You taught us.**[81]

When the Companions of the Prophet Muhammad (ﷺ) were asked about something that they did not know, they would say: "Allaah and His Messenger know best." This is only because of the perfection of their knowledge and their faith and their glorification of Allaah, and being far removed from embarking on matters beyond them.

3. Beware of accusing someone of disbelief or being sinful without proof.

Indeed it is a most dangerous matter for one to dare to accuse someone of disbelief or of being sinful without proof and authorisation from the Qur'aan and the *Sunnah* of the Prophet Muhammad (ﷺ). There is no doubt that this is insolence towards Allaah and His religion and it is also speaking about Him without knowledge. This is also in contradiction to the behaviour of the people of knowledge

---

81 Soorah al-Baqarah (2):32

and faith from among the pious predecessors, *radiyallaahu 'anhum.* May Allaah make us from amongst their followers in righteousness.

It has been authentically reported that the Prophet Muhammad (ﷺ) said: "*Whoever says to his brother, 'O kaafir!' It returns to one of them.*" He also said: "*Anyone who called his brother 'O kaafir!' Or 'O enemy of Allaah!' And it was not correct, it would return back to him.*"[82] i.e., whatever he said falls back on him.

This is a strong threat, warning the people of accusing others of disbelieving and being sinful, except when they have sure knowledge and understanding. This and other evidences are also a warning that one should be careful to guard his tongue, and only say, that which is good.

4. Beware of being hasty.

How many calamities, difficulties and problems have afflicted those who are hasty! The days and nights are going and leaving behind the traces and consequences of hastiness!

How much corruption and destruction and unpraiseworthy consequence have occurred because of partisanship and the following of desires? We ask Allaah to keep us safe from that.

5. Beware of partisanship to a group.

It is not permissible for one to blindly follow this person or that person, or the opinion of such and such a person. Nor should he follow blindly the methodology, or group of any individual.

---

82 *Saheeh al-Bukhaaree* [Eng. transl.8/80/no.125(b)] and [Eng. transl.8/44/no.71] p.36

Differing, it's effects and cure.

There is no doubt that differing is one of the greatest trials and calamities to befall the Muslim *Ummah*. It is one of the reasons why efforts are being wasted and truth is lost. Differing among Islamic groups and Islamic centres, harms the Islamic *da'wah*. The only way that they can succeed is to have a unification of goals and is that they all exert their efforts and work together towards the goal which will secure the power and glory of Islaam and the safety of the Muslims. It is necessary for every group, institution and community who want success in the Hereafter to help each other enjoin *al-Birr* (righteousness) and *taqwa* (piety). They should be sincere in their actions towards Allaah and their primary concern should be the victory of Allaah's *deen*, so that everyone can join together upon the truth and work upon what Allaah has said in His Book.

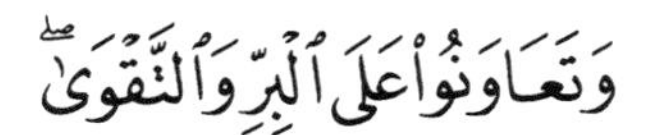

Help you one another in *al-Birr* and *at-Taqwa*.[83]

My advice for the *daa'ees* is that they should make sure that the actions should be done sincerely and purely for the sake of Allaah, the Most High, alone. They should help one another in *al-Birr* and *Taqwa* and agree to rule by the Qur'aan and *Sunnah* whenever a disagreement breaks out amongst them, in accordance to what Allaah says in the Qur'aan,

فَإِن تَنَٰزَعۡتُمۡ فِي شَيۡءٖ فَرُدُّوهُ إِلَى ٱللَّهِ وَٱلرَّسُولِ إِن كُنتُمۡ
تُؤۡمِنُونَ بِٱللَّهِ وَٱلۡيَوۡمِ ٱلۡأٓخِرِۚ ذَٰلِكَ خَيۡرٞ وَأَحۡسَنُ تَأۡوِيلًا ٥٩

83 Soorah al-Maa'idah (5):2

And if you differ in anything amongst yourselves, refer it to Allaah and His Messenger if you believe in Allaah and in the Last Day. That is better and more suitable for final determination.[84]

By this the goal will be one and the same and the efforts to search for success and warn away from following desires will be unified. Allaah, the Most High, says,

فَإِن لَّمْ يَسْتَجِيبُوا۟ لَكَ فَٱعْلَمْ
أَنَّمَا يَتَّبِعُونَ أَهْوَآءَهُمْ ۚ وَمَنْ أَضَلُّ مِمَّنِ ٱتَّبَعَ هَوَىٰهُ بِغَيْرِ
هُدًى مِّنَ ٱللَّهِ ۚ

But if they answer you not, they know that they only follow their own lusts, and who is more astray than one who follows his own lusts, without guidance from Allaah?[85]

Allaah says in the Qur'aan addressing His Prophet and His Messenger Daawood, *'alaiyhis-salaam,*

يَـٰدَاوُۥدُ إِنَّا جَعَلْنَـٰكَ خَلِيفَةً فِى ٱلْأَرْضِ فَٱحْكُم بَيْنَ ٱلنَّاسِ
بِٱلْحَقِّ وَلَا تَتَّبِعِ ٱلْهَوَىٰ فَيُضِلَّكَ عَن سَبِيلِ ٱللَّهِ ۚ

O Daawood! Verily We have placed you as a successor on earth, so judge you between men in truth and follow not your desire-for it will mislead you from the Path of Allaah.[86]

---

[84] Soorah an-Nisaa' (4):59

[85] Soorah al-Qasas (28):50

[86] Soorah Saad (38):26

Chapter 24
Beware of Supporting Someone Just Because his or her Opinion Agrees With Yours

The *deen* of Allaah must be the authority that judges everything. Beware of following your brother just because he agrees with you over an opinion and oppose another because he disagrees with you over an opinion or an issue. This is not being just or fair. We know that the *sahaabah* differed in issues, but this did not effect the good faith, support and love between them, *radiyallaahu 'anhum*. So the believer acts by Allaah's laws and he accepts and submits to the truth and he makes it precede everything else.

The believer should not oppress his brother, or act unjustly towards him if he differs with him over an opinion from the issues of *Ijtihaad*, in which the proofs may not be clear, or issues in which there may be differing interpretations of the text. He may have an excuse, so you must advise him and love the *khayr* (goodness) for him and do not allow the differing to induce and prompt aggression and discord between you. Do not enable the enemy to take advantage of you and your brother. And there is no movement or power except with Allaah, the Most High.

Chapter 25
Books for the *Daa'ee*

The greatest and most noble book which I recommend is the Book of Allaah, the Qur'aan, which contains no falsehood at all.

So I advise every *daa'ee* to Allaah and everyone who enjoins the good and forbids the evil, the guide, the instructor, the teacher, male or female, I advise them all to devote their attention to the Book of Allaah, the Most High, to reflect on it and to read it often. For indeed, the Book of Allaah is the origin and root of every good and the instructor and the guide to al good.

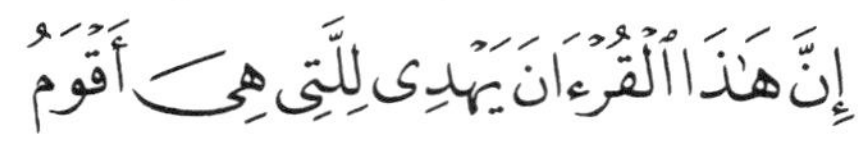

> **Indeed this Qur'aan guided to that which is most upright.**[87]

It is the guidance of Allaah and guides to the most upright path, the path of intellect and wisdom.

Therefore it is necessary for the *daa'ees* and those who enjoin the good and the teachers all to exert their efforts in reading the Qur'aan and reflecting on its meanings. This is how they will benefit tremendously and become qualified to give *da'wah* and teach by the help of Allaah.

Secondly I advise the *daa'ees* to adhere to the *Sunnah* and the knowledge and guidance that comes with it. The one who enjoins goodness and forbids the evil and the teacher male or female, must all consult the books of *hadeeth* and what the people have compiled in this field. This is so you can derive benefit from these works. The

---

[87] Soorah al-Israa' (17):9

most important and most authentic books of *hadeeth* are *Saheeh al-Bukhaaree* and *Saheeh Muslim*. Therefore one should refer back to them often, in order to derive benefit. In addition to these one may refer back to the other well-known books of *hadeeth*. Such as *al-Sunan al-Arbaa'a* (i.e., *Sunan Aboo Daawood, Sunan an-Nasaa'ee, Sunan at-Tirmidhee* and *Sunan Ibn Maajah*), *Muwatta Imaam Maalik, Sunan ad-Daarimee* as well as other well known books of *hadeeth* which the people of knowledge have advised us to refer back to. Such as, *al-Muntaqa lil-Majd* of Ibn Taymiyyah, *Riyaadh us-Saaliheen, Baloogh al-Maraam, 'Umdatul Hadeeth, Jaami'al 'Ilm wal Fadlahu* by Ibn 'Abdul-Barr, *Jaami'ul 'Uloom wal Hikm* by Haafidh Ibn Rajab and *Zaad al-Ma'aad* by the great scholar Ibn al-Qayyim as well as his other books like *'Alaam al-Muwaqi'een, Tareeq al-Hijratayn* and *Turuq al-Haakimiyyah*. He has mentioned many things concerning *da'wah* and ordering the good and forbidding the evil in these books. So the Muslims should benefit from them because they are excellent books by *Imaams* and Scholars, who are of crucial importance in this field and have excelled in their faith (*'aqeedah*) and who are greatly experienced.

Also of crucial importance is what Abul 'Abbaas Shaykhul-Islaam, Ibn Taymiyyah has written in the books: *Siyaasatush Sharee'ah, al-Hisbah* and *Minhaaj us-Sunnah.*

He is from the great Imaams who practised *da'wah* and excelled in it and Allaah, the Most High, made the *Ummah* benefit by it, the truth victorious through it, and it subdued innovations and their people. May Allaah, the Most High, reward him and his brothers from amongst the scholars for their patience, efforts and struggle, with the best reward he gives to the good doers. Indeed Allaah is the Most Generous!

I advise every Muslim, teacher and guide to devote their attention to these beneficial books, after paying attention to the Qur'aan and *Sunnah* of Prophet Mu<u>h</u>ammad (ﷺ). Likewise I advise them to read the books written on the subject by the *Imaams* of knowledge and guidance from the *Maalikee*, *Shaafi'ee* and *<u>H</u>anafee madhhabs* as well as the books of the *<u>H</u>anbalees*, of those who are well known for their knowledge, guidance and good *'aqeedah*.

The books written on this subject by the people of knowledge are aimed to help the *daa'ee* to be guided to that which he is ignorant about and towards a greater amount of knowledge.

Allaah, the Most High, says in the Qur'aan:

وَتَزَوَّدُوا۟ فَإِنَّ خَيْرَ ٱلزَّادِ ٱلتَّقْوَىٰ ۚ

> **And take provision (with you) for the journey, but the best provision is *at-taqwa.*** [88]

There is no doubt that educating oneself about the *deen* and gaining sure knowledge is from *taqwa*.

---

[88] Soorah al-Baqarah (2):197

Chapter 26
To Have a Good Opinion of the *Daa'ees* and How to Advise Them if They are Wrong.

Allaah orders us to avoid suspicion and has informed us that some of it is a sin when there is no proof for it and no legal evidence to support it.

It has been established in two authentic narrations, on the authority of Aboo Hurayrah, that Prophet Muhammad (ﷺ) said: "*Beware of adh-dhann (conjecture, suspicion) for verily it is the most untruthful speech.*"[89]

However all this does not prevent one from giving advice to the one who commits an error from among the people of knowledge, or the *daa'ee*, when he commits an error in his *da'wah*, his behaviour or in something that he does. Rather it is necessary to direct him towards goodness and guide him towards the truth in a good manner and not to defame him, have bad suspicion or by a harsh manner as this causes a repulsion of the truth rather than bringing him closer to it. We can see how Allaah, the Most High, told his two Messengers, *'alayhimas-salaam*, Moosaa and Haaroon to behave when He sent them to the worst and most disbelieving person of their time. Allaah, the Most High, tells them,

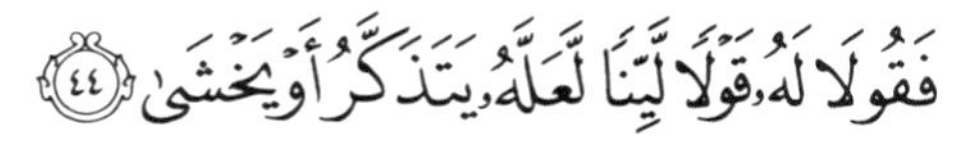

And speak to him mildly, perhaps he may accept admonition and fear Allaah.[90]

---

[89] *Saheeh al-Bukhaaree* [Eng. transl. 8/58/no.90] and Muslim [Eng. transl. 4/1361/ no.6214].

[90] Soorah Taa Haa (20):44

Chapter 27
When do we Excuse Each Other

Indeed, we must co-operate and agree with one another with respect to that which we are in agreement about in relation to aiding the truth, calling to it and warning against that which Allaah and Prophet Muhammad (ﷺ) have forbidden. As for excusing each other with regards to what we differ on, then this is not absolute and requires elaboration. On the issues of *ijtihaad*, when the proof is not clear, we must not refute one another. However in cases where someone contradicts the text of the Qur'aan and the *Sunnah*, then it is obligatory to refute the one who is doing this, with wisdom, a good sermon and argue in a way that is better, working in accordance with Allaah's saying,

وَتَعَاوَنُوا۟ عَلَى ٱلْبِرِّ وَٱلتَّقْوَىٰ ۖ وَلَا تَعَاوَنُوا۟
عَلَى ٱلْإِثْمِ وَٱلْعُدْوَٰنِ ۚ

> **Help you one another in *al-Birr* and *at-Taqwa* but do not help one another in sin and transgression.**[91]

Allaah, the Most High, also says in the Qur'aan,

وَٱلْمُؤْمِنُونَ وَٱلْمُؤْمِنَٰتُ بَعْضُهُمْ
أَوْلِيَآءُ بَعْضٍ ۚ يَأْمُرُونَ بِٱلْمَعْرُوفِ وَيَنْهَوْنَ عَنِ ٱلْمُنكَرِ

> **The believers men and women are *awliyaa* (helpers, supporters) of one another they enjoin the good and forbid the evil.**[92]

---

[91] Soorah al-Maa'idah 5:2

[92] Soorah at-Tawbah (9):71

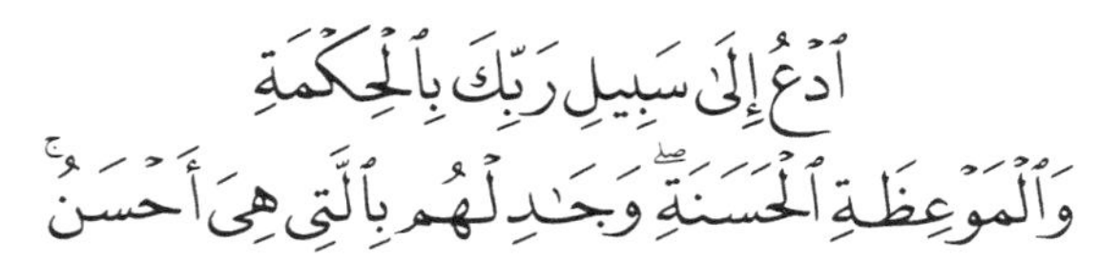

Invite (mankind O Muhammad (ﷺ)) to the way of your Lord with wisdom and fair preaching and argue with them in a way that is better.[93]

The Prophet Muhammad (ﷺ) said: "*Whoever among you sees munkar (evil) then let him change it with his hand, and if he is not able to then with his tongue, and if he is not able to then in his heart.*"[94]

Therefore it is not befitting when the Muslims are united and their speech is one and upon the truth, and are clinging to the rope of Allaah, to not refute the evil and whoever practises it or believes in it from among the *Soofees* and others. But rather by acting in accordance with the order to hold onto the rope of Allaah, the Most High, they should enjoin the good and forbid the evil. One must also clarify the truth to whoever strays from it, or who thinks that the opposite of the truth is correct, with evidences from the *Sharee'ah* so that they all come altogether upon the truth and reject what opposes it.

Allaah, the Most High, says in the Qur'aan,

---

93 Soorah an-Nahl (16):125

94 *Saheeh Muslim* [Eng. transl. 1/33/no.79].

Help you one another in *al-Birr* and *at-Taqwa* but do not help one another in sin and transgression.[95]

Let their arise out of you a group of people inviting to all that is good and enjoining the good and forbidding the evil. And it is they who are successful.[96]

So when the people of truth kept silent about clarifying the error of the wrong doers and their mistakes, they didn't fulfil the order of Allaah, the Most High, by inviting and ordering the good and forbidding evil. We know the result of the sin of remaining silent and not refuting evil is that the wrong-doer remains on his error and continues to contradict the truth. This opposes what Allaah, the Most High, has legislated, which is to advise and co-operate with each other upon goodness and enjoin the good and forbid the evil and Allaah, the Most High, is the Guardian of success.

---

95 Soorah al-Maa'idah (5):2

96 Soorah Aal-'Imraan 3:104

Chapter 28
Using Visits for Giving *Da'wah*

If we visit each other for the sake of guiding, advising and cooperating upon goodness then this is a good thing. Prophet Muhammad (ﷺ) has told us: "*Allaah, the Most High, says: 'My Love is guaranteed for those people who love each other for my sake, who visit each other for my sake, who sit together for my sake and who give things to each other for my sake'.*" Collected by Imaam Maalik, *rahimahullaah*, with a *saheeh isnaad*.[97] The Prophet (ﷺ) said: "*Seven people are shaded by Allaah, the Most High, on the day when there is no shade except His.*"[98] He mentioned that amongst these people are two people who love each other for the sake of Allaah, the Most High, and they meet and part upon this. This applies to both men and women.

---

97 *Muwatta Imaam Maalik.*

98 *Saheeh al-Bukhaaree* [Eng. transl. 1/356/no.629] and Muslim [Eng. transl. 2/493/no.2248].

Chapter 29
Utilising Ones Time During the Holidays to Give *Da'wah*

I advise all the teachers to utilise their time in their holidays in setting up study circles in mosques, and lectures, there is a strong need for this. Likewise I advise them all to tour the countries which need *da'wah* according to their ability. They should visit the Islamic centres and Islamic minorities in these countries, to give *da'wah* and guidance by teaching the Muslims about that which they are ignorant of concerning their *deen* and encouraging them to co-operate amongst themselves by advising each other with the truth and being patient. They should also encourage the students present there to adhere to their religion and to concentrate on the reason they were brought into existence and warn them against the causes of deviation. They should advise them to devote themselves to the Noble Qur'aan, by memorising it, reciting it, and reflecting upon it as well as acting in accordance to the pure *Sunnah*, to memorise it, study it and work in accordance with it, also.

I ask Allaah, the Most High, to make the Muslims successful, old and young, the teachers and students, the scholars and the general public, in everything that is in their best interests, towards happiness and success in this world and in the Hereafter. Indeed Allaah, the Most High, is the Most Generous.

Chapter 30
The Role of Women in Giving *Da'wah*

Just like the man, it is necessary for the woman to give *da'wah*, order the good and forbid the evil. This is because the texts in the Noble Qur'aan and the pure *Sunnah* of the Prophet Muhammad (ﷺ) indicate towards this and, this has also been clarified by the people of knowledge.

Therefore the woman, just like the man, should call to Allaah and order the good and forbid the evil in ways and ettiquettes prescribed by the *Sharee'ah*. She must not let insults or mockery from the people, cause her to become anxious and impatient, and thus turn her away from giving *da'wah*. Rather she must be tolerant and patient.

Even if she is subject to any sort of mockery, insults or abuse from the people, she must take care to be a virtuous and good example. She must maintain her *hijaab* from strange men and stay away from free mixing.

She should be careful when giving *da'wah*, to stay away from that which has been made unlawful for her. If she gives *da'wah* to men, she should do so in full *hijaab*, and not in seclusion with anyone. When giving *da'wah* to the women, she should do so with wisdom. She should be just, upright and pure in her character and in her behaviour. This is so that no one can raise objections against her and say: 'Why don't you start with yourself first!'

The woman should not wear clothing that will display her beauty and her charms, or be alluring in her speech. This has been forbidden, and causes *fitnah* for the people. Rather she should concentrate on giving *da'wah* in a way that does not harm her religion or her reputation.

The Muslim woman has a high status in Islaam and holds a large influence over the lives of every Muslim. She holds the primary role in education towards the building of a righteous and pure society, if she follows the guidance in the Qur'aan and the *Sunnah* of Prophet Muhammad (ﷺ). This is because, sticking firmly to these two sources keeps every Muslim (male and female) away from being misguided or straying in any matter. The misguidance and deviation of nations only happens when the *Ummah* is distant from the path of Allaah and what his Prophets and Messengers have brought. The Prophet Muhammad (ﷺ) said: "*I have left you with two things, and if you hold onto them both you will not go astray, and they are the Book of Allaah and my Sunnah.*"[99]

The importance of the woman as a mother, a wife, and a sister and as a daughter has been mentioned in the Noble Qur'aan, as well as her rights, responsibilities and her duties. The pure *Sunnah* of Prophet Muhammad (ﷺ) elaborates on this. The unique stance adopted by Khadeejah had the greatest influence in calming the Prophet Muhammad's (ﷺ) fears after his first experience with the angel Jibraa'eel, *'alaiyhis-salaam*, when he came down to him with the revelation for the first time in the cave of Hiraa. The Prophet Muhammad (ﷺ) came to her trembling with fear and said: "*Cover me, cover me, I am afraid for myself.*" She comforted him, saying: "*Be happy, Allaah will never harm you. You are the one who visits relatives. You always speak the truth and are always helping everyone. You give to the poor and are generous with your guest, and help when calamities befall them.*"[100]

---

99 *Muwatta* of Imaam Maalik.

100 *Saheeh al-Bukhaaree* [Eng. transl. 1/2-5/no.3] and Muslim [Eng. transl. 1/96/no.301].

Chapter 31
How Should the Female *Daa'ee* Advise the Females Who Display their Charms and Beauty

One should advise her sister that Allaah has made it incumbent upon her to keep away from mixing freely and to veil herself. One must draw her attention to the order in the Qur'aan that tells the Muslim woman that she must maintain her *hijaab* in front of men that are not her *mahrams*.

Allaah says in the Qur'aan,

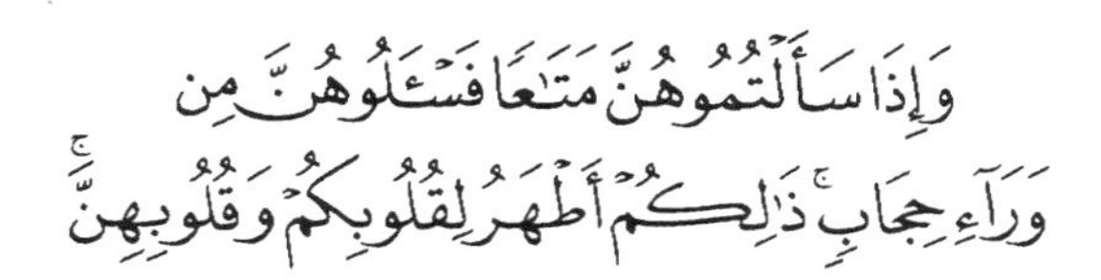

And when you ask (his wives) for anything you want, ask them from behind a screen, that is purer for your hearts and for their hearts.[101]

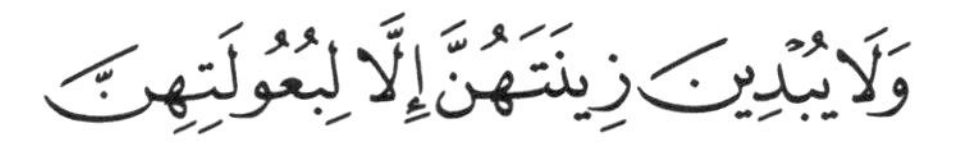

...and do not show off their adornment except to their husbands...[102]

So one should present the relevant verses and *ahaadeeth* which clarify what is required from the Muslim woman, warning her away from doing that which contradicts the pure Islamic ruling.

---

[101] Soorah al-Ahzaab (33):53

[102] Soorah an-Noor (24):31

One should make it clear to her sisters that Allaah has made it incumbent upon us all to be wary of what He has made *haraam*, and to help each other in *Birr* (righteousness) and *Taqwa* (piety), and to advise each other with the truth and be patient upon it.

Chapter 32
How do we Give *Da'wah* to the People of Innovation and the *Soofees*

It is obligatory upon the scholars of Islaam to spread the *deen* of Allaah amongst the people. They must clarify the falsehood and superstitions that the people of *bid'ah* and *Soofees* are upon. They should also present and explain to these people the beautiful *Sunnah* of the Prophet Muhammad (ﷺ) and the clear and noble path, with evidence from the Qur'aan and the *Sunnah*. They should be informed of their mistakes in a good, kind and thoughtful manner, with clear evidences, strong proof and irrefutable argument. The scholars must express themselves clearly without violence or severity and argue with them in a way that is good.

Thus these misguided people will come to know about the truth and then be guided to that which is right, until they leave the superstitions, *shirk* and *bid'ah* they are upon, which are not based on guidance and sure knowledge.

The truth is the goal of persistent search for the believer so when he finds it he holds on to it.

Allaah says in the Qur'aan,

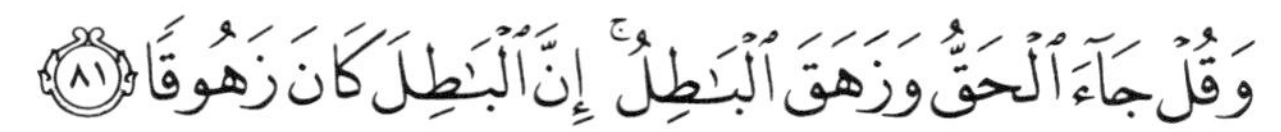

And say: truth has come and falsehood has vanished. Surely falsehood is ever bound to vanish.[103]

The Prophet Muhammad (ﷺ) said: "*Whoever does something that we have not ordered in the religion, it is rejected*."[104]

---

103 Soorah al-Israa' (17):81

104 *Saheeh Muslim.*

Chapter 33
How to Fight Destructive Thoughts

It is only through beneficial knowledge, (derived from the Qur'aan and the *Sunnah*), that Allaah can be worshipped, His right be given to Him, His *deen* be spread and that destructive thoughts, misleading *da'wah* and corruptive thoughts be fought.

Thus ones duties cannot be performed and Allaah cannot be feared except with knowledge. Through it one discovers the truths present in the Qur'aan and the *Sunnah* of the Prophet Muhammad (ﷺ).

Allaah, the Most High, says in the Qur'aan,

And no example do they bring but We reveal to you the truth and the better explanation thereof.[105]

So everything that the people of falsehood present in their misguiding *da'wah* and in directing others to it in false deceptive ways, causing doubt in others about what Allaah and the Prophet Muhammad (ﷺ) have said, one should refute and shows it's errors with what Allaah and the Prophet Muhammad (ﷺ) have said, in clear words complete explanation and with valuable proofs and argument. This will fill the hearts of the people and support the truth. This is only because the knowledge taken from the Qur'aan and the pure *Sunnah* is Knowledge which comes from the Wise and All Knowing, the Most High.

He Knows the conditions of the servants and their problems as well as the evil or sound thoughts within them. He also knows what the

---

105 Soorah al-Furqaan (25):33

people of falsehood will bring throughout the times. Allaah knows all of this, and so He sent down the Qur'aan to clarify the truth from the falsehood and to establish the proofs and arguments about what the Messengers called to. His Messenger Prophet Muhammad (ﷺ) was sent down with guidance and the religion of truth. His Noble Book was sent down, to explain everything and as a guidance, a mercy and glad tidings for the Muslims.

Indeed the people of falsehood only work, and are active when there is a lack of knowledge and ignorance is prevalent and at a time when there is no one who refers back to what Allaah and the Prophet Muhammad (ﷺ) have said. So at a time like this they will be like lions against others who are not from amongst them and be active in their falsehood. This is because of the lack of those who the people of falsehood fear, from amongst the people of truth, *eemaam* and deep insight.

Allaah has mentioned everything in His Book, generally in some passages and elaborately in others.

Allaah says in the Qur'aan,

وَنَزَّلْنَا عَلَيْكَ ٱلْكِتَـٰبَ تِبْيَـٰنًا لِّكُلِّ شَىْءٍ

> **...We have sent down to you the Book as an exposition of everything...**[106]

These are the words of the All-Wise, the Most High.

---

106 Soorah an-Nahl (16):89

Chapter 34
Giving *Da'wah* to Those Influenced by Deviant Culture

The *daa'ee* must clarify the errors and *bid'ah* that influences the people from their schools of thought and the paths which they follow, as well as the environments which they live in. Thus, he explains to them the things which contradict the Islamic *Sharee'ah*, practised in the groups and communities which they live in. He should call them to refer everything that seems obscure and dubious to them, back to the just scale and that is the Qur'aan and the *Sunnah*. Whatever agrees with both of them, or with one of them is considered as binding. And whatever contradicts them, reject it, no matter who says it.

Chapter 35
How Can We Confront Intellectual Attack.

We must confront the intellectual onslaught represented in the radio, books, newspapers, magazines and writings which the Muslim communities in our present time have been afflicted with. The Muslim male and female spend most of their time with such, despite the fact that they contain deadly poison and misleading propagation most of the time. Therefore confronting this is a very important issue if we want to protect Islaam and the Islamic culture from its conspiracies and evil.

The *daa'ees* and the defenders of Islaam must devote their time in writing beneficial researches, articles, periodicals and give *da'wah*. They should respond to different types of cultural attack and expose its defects and clarify its falseness. The enemies have gathered now and are preparing all their efforts and abilities to establish different organisations and various ways to scheme and plot against the Muslims and deceive them.

Therefore we must counter attack these enemies. We must refute and disapprove of their networks, expose them, and present Islaam as a faith, belief, legal system and a social and moral system. This should be done in a way that will make the people learn it, through good methods suitable for the age, and with wisdom and good admonition, arguing in a way that is best. We should use all the methods of the media, according to the resources available and our ability.

The *deen* of Islaam is a complete *deen*, which contains all good. It is the source of happiness for all mankind, and helps us in achieving righteous prosperity, sound progression, security, tranquillity and a noble life and victory in this life and in the Hereafter.

Chapter 36
How do we Confront the Efforts of the Enemies of Islaam

The leaders and the scholars should exert efforts to enlighten and direct the population of Muslims and combat the efforts of the enemies of Islaam, by retaliating with their own efforts.

The Muslim *Ummah* is an *Ummah* that has been entrusted with this religion and has the responsibility of conveying it. If we are careful to arm our boys and girls in Islamic societies, with knowledge, understanding and comprehension of Islamic Jurisprudence and accustom them to apply these things from a small age, then we will not fear, by the permission of Allaah, the Most High, as long as they continue holding onto the *deen* of Allaah, glorifying it, following its laws, and fighting that which contradicts it. And indeed their enemies will fear them.

Allaah, the Most High, says in the Qur'aan,

يَـٰٓأَيُّهَا ٱلَّذِينَ ءَامَنُوٓا۟ إِن تَنصُرُوا۟ ٱللَّهَ يَنصُرْكُمْ وَيُثَبِّتْ أَقْدَامَكُمْ ﴿٧﴾

O you who believe! If you help Allaah, He will help you and make your foothold firm.[107]

وَإِن تَصْبِرُوا۟ وَتَتَّقُوا۟ لَا يَضُرُّكُمْ كَيْدُهُمْ شَيْـًٔا ۗ إِنَّ ٱللَّهَ بِمَا يَعْمَلُونَ مُحِيطٌ ﴿١٢٠﴾

If you remain patient and become *al-Muttaqoon* (pious) not the least harm will their cunning do to you. Surely Allaah surrounds all that they do.[108]

---

107 Soorah Muhammad (47):7

108 Soorah Aal-'Imraan (3):120

There are many verses in the Qur'aan which convey this message. The most important factor for us in fighting against the efforts of our enemies is raising and preparing a generation that knows the reality of Islaam. This can be achieved through guidance, taking care of the house and family, the method of educating them, the media and improvement of the society.

In addition to this is the role of steering and guiding which needs to be taken by the Muslim leadership, perservering in beneficial work and continually reminding the people that which will benefit them and make the belief within them grow and flourish.

Chapter 37
Being Concerned About the Islamic Minorities

We have read and heard in the news much about our Muslim brothers in communities where the majority of the population is non-Muslim. They are under authorities which imposes restrictions on them, in practising their religion and establishing their rites of worship, in order to distance them from their religion through compulsion and in other ways.

We ask Allaah to firmly establish these Muslim minorities, and indeed all the Muslims upon Islaam and keep them safe from the plots of the enemies.

There is no doubt that they are in a seriously vulnerable situation. Because of this situation, these Islamic minorities need all the help, co-operation and assistance, from the political sphere and this is specially from the Islamic governments from the Arab world as well as others that have special concern for Islaam. They have relations with these nations through sending delegates, despatching messages and urging their embassies to act, or any other similar methods that will help their brothers in these regions. This will raise the morale of the minorities and make the (oppressing) nations realise that these minorities have brothers from the same faith, who are concerned about their situation and who follow their news.

If Allaah, the Most High wills, the injustice and oppression will then be lifted from the Muslims when these oppressing nations and others begin to realise that behind the minority of Muslims is a nation which feels their pain and is interested in their affairs. As a result they will give into their requests and will raise their hand from oppressing them, especially when the majority of these nations need Islamic countries for their economic and other affairs.

There is no doubt that the minority of Muslims everywhere are in urgent need of moral support and material help and resources to build mosques and schools that will help them in their Islamic work.

So therefore it is obligatory upon every Muslim to help in accordance to his ability. *Daa'ees* should be sent to them to teach them the true *'aqeedah* (belief) as well as the Arabic language, because many of them are very ignorant about matters concerning their *deen*.

Chapter 38
After you Have Done What is Required of you Then Don't Worry

If the people of knowledge and deep understanding and *eemaan* spread the reality of Islaam, help the people perceive the *Sharee'ah* of Allaah, and clarify the proofs concerning that, then after this Allaah will guide whom He wills.

As a result the scholars of Islaam would have treated people well and informed them about what is obligatory upon them, and have carried out their duty. Then after this if one goes astray, (after the knowledge has been conveyed to him), then his matter returns to Allaah, Allaah has promised the Fire it's fill and has promised Paradise it's fill.

Allaah, the Most High, says in the Qu'raan,

> **Not upon you (Prophet Mu<u>h</u>ammad (ﷺ)) is their guidance, but Allaah guides whom He wills.**[109]

So it is only obligatory for the people of knowledge to convey the message, explain it, give a clear insight and establish the proofs, and then be patient after that, and Allaah will guide whom He wills.

---

109 Soorah al-Baqarah (2):272

Chapter 39
The Final Advice

Finally I advise my Muslim brothers and sisters in Islaam, to have *taqwa* (fear) of Allaah in all matters and to be firmly established on His *deen*. They should fear Him wherever they are and be heedful of Him. They should take account of themselves, and be careful not to leave what Allaah has made obligatory upon them, nor to commit a sin.

I advise them to co-operate upon *Birr* and *Taqwa* and to be sincere to each other and advise each other with the truth patience and wherever they are.

I also advise them to gain a deep and good understanding of the *deen* and attend circles of knowledge and question the scholars. The Prophet Muhammad (ﷺ) said in an authentic tradition: "*When Allaah wants good for someone he grants him an understanding of the deen.*"[110] He also said: "*Whoever treads a path, seeking knowledge, Allaah will make the path to paradise easy for him.*"[111]

So we know that learning knowledge by searching for it is one of the most important tasks that a Muslim should undertake.

I ask Allaah, the Most High, with His great and His magnificent attributes to make the Muslims successful wherever they are in all that pleases Him, the Most High.

I ask Allaah to make those in charge of the Muslims and their leaders, upright and honest and to guide everyone to the straight path.

---

110 *Saheeh al-Bukhaaree* [Eng. transl. 1/61/no.71].

111 *Saheeh Muslim* [Eng. transl. 4/1417/no.6518].

I ask Him to make their leaders and their aides successful, and all their people to rule by the Islamic laws and rulings. And to be ruled by them, to be firmly established upon them, and to advise each other upon them, and to beware of and forbid that which contradicts them.

Indeed He is the All Hearer, the Ever Watchful.

Praise be to Allaah, the Most High, and peace and blessing upon our Prophet Muhammad and upon his family and his Companions.

Glossary

Aayah (pl. Aayaat): a Sign of Allaah; a verse of the Qur'aan.
Aayaat: See *Aayah.*
'Abd: worshipper.
Aboo (Abee, Abaa): father of; used as a means of identification.
'Alayhis-salaam: "may Allaah protect and preserve him." It is said after the name of a Prophet of Allaah or after the name of an angel.
Ahaadeeth: See *Hadeeth.*
Ansaar: "Helpers"; the Muslims of Madeenah who supported the Muslims who migrated from Makkah.
'Aqeedah: that which binds or that which is rooted in the heart; the principles and details of belief.
Companions (Ar. *Sahaabah*): the Muslims who saw the Prophet (ﷺ) and died upon Islaam.
Daa'ee: One who performs *da'wah.*
Da'wah: invitation; call to Allaah.**Deen**: way of life prescribed by Allaah i.e. Islaam.
Eemaan: faith; to affirm all that was revealed to the Messenger (ﷺ), affirming with the heart, testifying with the tongue and acting with the limbs. The actions of the limbs are from the completeness of *eemaan*. Faith increases with obedience to Allaah and decreases with disobedience.
Fard 'Ayn: 'an individual duty' i.e., obligatory on every individual.
Fard Kifaayah: collective obligation - if fulfilled by a part of the community then the rest are not obliged to fulfil it.
Fataawa: see *fatwa.*
Fatwa (pl. Fataawa): religious verdict.
Fiqh: the understanding and application of the *Sharee'ah* from its sources.
Fitrah: the natural disposition that one is born upon..
Hadeeth (pl. **Ahaadeeth**): narration concerning the utterances of the Prophet (ﷺ), his actions or an attribute of his.
Hajj: Pilgrimage to Makkah.

Halaal: permitted under the *Sharee'ah*.
Haraam: prohibited under the *Sharee'ah*.
Hijrah: the migration of the Prophet (ﷺ) from Makkah to al-Madeenah; migration of the Muslims from the land of the disbelievers to the lands of the Muslims.
Ibn: son of; used as a means of identification.
'Ilm: knowledge.
Imaam: leader; leader in *salaah*, knowledge or *fiqh*; leader of a state.
Isnaad: the chain of narrators linking the collector of the saying to the person quoted.
Jihaad: striving and fighting to make the Word of Allaah supreme.
Jinn: a creation of Allaah created from smokeless fire.
Jumu'ah: Friday.
Kaafir (pl. **Kuffaar**): a rejector of Islaam i.e. a disbeliever.
Kufr: disbelief.
Masaajid: see *masjid.*
Masjid (pl. Masaajid): mosque.
Muhaajir (pl. Muhaajiroon/Muhaajireen): One who migrates from the lands of the disbelievers to the land of the Muslims for the sake of Allaah.
Muhaajireen: see *muhaajir.*
Muhaajiroon: see *muhaajir.*
Mushrik: one who worships others along with Allaah or ascribes one or more of Allaah's attributes to other than Him; one who commits *shirk*.
Radiyallaahu 'anhu/'anhaa/'anhum/'anhumaa: may Allaah be pleased with him/her/them/both of them.
Rahimahullaah/Rahimahumullaah: may Allaah bestow His mercy upon him/them.
Ramadaan: the ninth month of the Islamic calendar, in which the Muslims fast.
Saheeh: correct; an authentic narration.
Salaat: prescribed prayer (e.g. the five obligatory prayers); prayers upon the Prophet (ﷺ).

Salaf: predecessors; the early Muslims; the Muslims of the first three generations: the *Companions*, the *Successors* and their successors.
Shahaadah: to bear witness (that none has the right to be worshipped except Allaah and Muhammad (ﷺ) is His Messenger); Martyrdom.
Shaykh: scholar.
Shaytaan: Satan.
Sharee'ah: the Divine code of Law.
Shirk: associating partners with Allaah; compromising any aspect of *tawheed.*
Soorah: a Chapter of the Qur'aan.
Sunnah: in its broadest sense, the entire *Deen* which the Prophet (ﷺ) came with and taught, i.e. all matters of belief, rulings, manners and actions which were conveyed by the *Companions.* It also includes those matters which the Prophet (ﷺ) established by his sayings, actions and tacit approval - as opposed to *bid'ah* (innovation).
sunnah: an action of the Prophet (ﷺ).
Tafseer: explanation of the Qur'aan.
Taqwaa: "*taqwaa* is acting in obedience to Allaah, hoping for His mercy upon light from Him and *taqwaa* is leaving acts of disobedience, out of fear of Him, upon light from Him."
Tawheed: Allaah is the only Lord of creation, He alone, is their provider and sustainer, Allaah has Names and Attributes that none of the creation share and Allaah is to be singled out for worship, alone. *Tawheed* is maintaining the Oneness of Allaah in all the above mentioned categories. Islaam makes a clear distinction between the Creator and the created.
Umm: mother of; used as a means of identification.
Ummah: "nation"; the Muslims as a group.
'Umrah: the lesser pilgrimage (to Makkah).
Usool: the fundamentals.